Kate Naito, CPDT-KA, MS

Ⓑ Ⓚ Ⓛ Ⓝ MANNERS™

CompanionHouse Books™ is an imprint of Fox Chapel Publishers International Ltd.

Project Team
Vice President-Content: Christopher Reggio
Editor: Amy Deputato
Copy Editor: Laura Taylor
Design: Mary Ann Kahn
Index: Elizabeth Walker

ISBN 978-1-62187-125-5

Library of Congress Cataloging-in-Publication Data

Names: Naito, Kate, author.
Title: BKLN manners : positive training solutions for your unruly urban dog /
    by Kate Naito, CPDT-KA.
Description: Mount Joy, PA : CompanionHouse Books, [2018] | Includes index. |
    Identifiers: LCCN 2017052685 (print) | LCCN 2017059370 (ebook) | ISBN
    9781621871767 (ebook) | ISBN 9781621871255 (softcover)
Subjects: LCSH: Dogs--Training.
Classification: LCC SF431 (ebook) | LCC SF431 .N35 2018 (print) | DDC
    636.7/0835--dc23
LC record available at https://lccn.loc.gov/2017052685

This book has been published with the intent to provide accurate and authoritative information in regard to the subject matter within. While every precaution has been taken in the preparation of this book, the author and publisher expressly disclaim any responsibility for any errors, omissions, or adverse effects arising from the use or application of the information contained herein. The techniques and suggestions are used at the reader's discretion and are not to be considered a substitute for veterinary care or personal dog training advice. If you suspect a medical or behavioral problem, contact your veterinarian or a qualified dog trainer.

Fox Chapel Publishing
903 Square Street
Mount Joy, PA 17552

Fox Chapel Publishers International Ltd.
7 Danefield Road, Selsey (Chichester)
West Sussex PO20 9DA, U.K.

www.facebook.com/companionhousebooks

We are always looking for talented authors. To submit an idea, please send a brief inquiry to acquisitions@foxchapelpublishing.com.

Printed and bound in China
20 19 18 17   2 4 6 8 10 9 7 5 3 1

CONTENTS

Preface   About BKLN Manners™ - 4

Introduction   It's a Mad World - 8

Chapter 1   Think Positive - 15

Chapter 2   Training: First Things First - 31

Chapter 3   **B** Barking - 39

Chapter 4   **K** Knocking People Over - 67

Chapter 5   **L** Leash-Walking Problems - 83

Chapter 6   **N** Naughty When Alone - 131

Chapter 7   More Useful Training for Urban Dogs - 153

Chapter 8   Additional Considerations for Urban Dog Owners - 175

               Conclusion - 196

               Appendix - 197

               Index - 218

               Photo Credits - 223

               About the Author - 224

Preface

ABOUT
B K L N
MANNERS™

As a dog trainer in Brooklyn, New York, I've learned that diversity is not limited to people. The dogs I work with every day run the gamut: snorting French Bulldogs, athletic Border Collies, rescue dogs from nearly every continent, designer dogs like Maltipoos to Puggles, blind and deaf dogs, and the list goes on. While these dogs may appear quite different, there is a common theme among them. When their owners contact me for help, nearly every request emphasizes the word *stop*. "Max needs to stop pulling." "I want Molly to stop eating garbage on the street." "I wish Sam would stop barking at noises in my building's hallway." And, being an urban dweller, I understand these very normal human concerns. None of us wants to get complaints because the dog's barking has been waking up the neighbors, and you can extract a half-eaten bagel from your dog's slimy jaws only so many times before losing it.

Prior to becoming a trainer, I was that exasperated owner bemoaning my dog's out-of-control barking and embarrassing leash-walking habits. My dog Batman, a then-young Chihuahua mix, had the typical vociferous Chihuahua reaction whenever our doorbell (or even the neighbor's) rang, and he spent most of our walks practicing for the Iditarod, doing his best to drag me down the street. I tried using the methods of training I'd grown up with, which emphasized

being a confident leader to my dog and "correcting" him when necessary. However, I wasn't actually feeling self-assured in my leadership abilities, and both my dog and I became confused and frustrated, eventually giving up on training because it seemed that only certain people had the necessary character to handle a dog properly—and I wasn't one of them.

Daily walks had become so full of miserable leash corrections that the mere sight of the leash sent my poor pup into hiding under the bed. I felt terrible. It wasn't until I took a leash manners class with Sarah Westcott, founder of Doggie Academy, that I realized I could replace Batman's rude behaviors with polite ones without using punishment. I remember the fourth and final class, during which the dog-and-handler duos walked around a city block full of the usual obstacles: bags of garbage awaiting pickup, discarded pizza crusts, workmen smoking on their breaks, kids whizzing by on scooters. The entire time, Batman only had eyes for me. There were no

leash corrections, no harsh words, but rather the occasional treat for polite walking and gentle cues to tell my dog to leave those obstacles alone. Even better than the loose leash walking itself was the new appreciation I had for my dog. We were communicating and walking together as a team rather than fighting each other. Those four classes changed everything.

Shortly thereafter, I pursued a career in dog training with Sarah as my mentor, and together we've worked to adapt tried-and-true positive training techniques to the unique needs of our busy urban clientele. So as you leave your apartment, cringing because your dog is howling like a maniac, or as you get dragged from one shrub to the next on your walks, remember that I was once there, too. And now I'm here to help.

Many dogs have learned basic obedience but still have trouble in their daily lives with barking at noises, jumping on people, walking on leash, and engaging in naughty behavior when left alone. Learning the basics is useless if you can't apply those skills to real-life situations, so I developed a group class at the Brooklyn Dog Training Center called *BKLN Manners*™ in 2016. As both a class and a book, *BKLN Manners*™ aims to teach you a few simple behaviors and give you the tools to practice them methodically so that ultimately your dog will be able to remain calm and polite even when faced with the perpetual distractions our urban environment throws at us. With consistency and practice, it's possible that your dog can greet strangers without jumping into their arms, walk through a crowded farmers' market on a loose leash, or accompany you to an outdoor café without stealing anyone's sandwich.

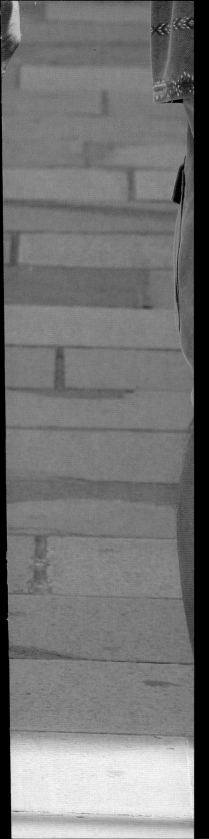

IT'S A MAD WORLD

Every dog trainer has certain clients she'll never forget. Pogo, the aptly named Goldendoodle puppy who came to his new Brooklyn family fully equipped with an internal trampoline, still stands out. When guests came through the front door, Pogo introduced himself with WWE body-slams and turned their sleeves into fishnet from all his playful biting. When the family left for work, Pogo took to howling and thrashing so intensely in his crate that neighbors above, below, and on both sides were complaining. His leash-walking acrobatics entertained passersby with a free Cirque du Soleil performance, though sometimes he took a break to help rid the Brooklyn sidewalks of their ubiquitous chicken bones and food wrappers.

Pogo's kind but exasperated humans had raised dogs before, but not one like this. Never a Goldendoodle, and never in a city. I awoke one morning to their tearful late-night voicemail: "He's crazy! This is not normal! He's not like this when we go to our country home. My vet thinks he needs to be medicated." And I can only imagine that Pogo, just doing what Doodles do, was thinking the same thing about his humans. In fact, Pogo was perfectly normal; it was his humans' world, with its leashes and doorbells and off-limits chicken bones, that was crazy.

Normal is subjective. That holds true for people from different backgrounds or cultures, and even more so for different species. Take the concept of personal space. Imagine you are standing in line at the post office, with a gentleman you've never met in front of you. A typical American will put roughly an arm's length of space between him- or herself and the gentleman in front; any closer than that would begin to feel uncomfortable. People from Mumbai might put only a few inches between individuals, with each person close enough to feel the breath of the person behind. (Americans, are you cringing yet?) And if Pogo were in that line, well, he'd jump right up onto that man's shoulders and slobber all over his back. The thing is, there is no right or wrong here, no good or bad, just different interpretations of what normal means. The problem for dogs is that they're participants in our world, and we expect them to follow our rules—and what crazy rules they must seem to be. Consider these examples:

City streets offer a lot of distractions for dogs.

YOU'RE THINKING:	YOUR DOG IS THINKING:
"I've only got ten minutes to walk the dog before work, so he'd better stop sniffing and just do his business."	"Walk on a rope at a slow human pace, not even stopping to eat that week-old discarded chicken wing? This stinks. Let's play! And, ahem, why are you staring at me while I poop?"
"Samson, please don't knock over Grandma when she comes through the door. Sit! Sit! Sit!"	"Finally, some excitement! Everybody, let's jump up and make some noise!"
"If my neighbors complain about Leroy barking out the window one more time, I'm in trouble."	"You guys! There's a dog on the sidewalk! Don't you hear me? A dog! Why aren't you listening? Hurry, come look!"

When Pogo's exhausted family left me that late-night voicemail, they said something that stuck with me: "He's not like this when we go to our country home." This reveals how the problem is not the dog himself; rather, has to do with the circumstances into which we put the dog.

When I was growing up in rural Connecticut, we rarely had to deal with problems such as incessant barking or difficult leash walking. Our family dog, a Golden Retriever mix who just wandered into our lives one day (and who I named Cindy as a tribute to Cyndi Lauper, whose style I shamelessly emulated), lived what most dogs would consider a "normal" lifestyle. She chose to stay outside from morning until evening, wandering around the property and interacting with other dogs and livestock while we humans were at school or work. Cindy had the autonomy to walk, poop, and sleep when she liked, and, as with most of the other dogs in our area, she developed good social skills on her own. That's not to say she was friendly to everyone, but if she didn't like certain people or other dogs, she had the freedom to simply avoid them or give them ample warning that they should stay away. Because of this, confrontations were infrequent.

Of course, there were certain risks to leaving dogs unsupervised, and Cindy's playmates were occasionally involved in accidents with cars or other animals. (Were I to live that lifestyle again, I would take more precautions than we did back then.) But, in general, these dogs lived happy, easygoing lives. The only time we ever used a leash on Cindy was to go to the vet. I'm sure her leash skills were horrific, but in the context of a rural lifestyle, it really didn't matter. Did she bark at the doorbell? Well, I don't think we even had a doorbell, and she was outside anyway, ready to size up whoever walked over.

In my early twenties, I moved to a cramped Boston apartment after college, and I immediately adopted a three-legged *sato* (Puerto Rican stray dog) who, despite the indignity of my naming her Three, became my doggie soul mate. In the city, I saw dogs put into a very different lifestyle. Three's routine was the polar opposite of Cindy's. My Boston life was busy, structured, and stressful, and somehow I expected this scrappy little street dog to adapt to a confined lifestyle. Though she did adjust remarkably well, I certainly went through my fair share of replacing chewed furniture, scrubbing pee stains, and regularly extracting dead animals from Three's jaws. I also learned what happens when, due to the restraint of the leash, dogs are forced to face what scares them and aren't able to engage in the normal reaction of *fight or flight*. Three, unable to practice *flight* by walking away from triggers like moving cars or children, turned to *fight*.

She felt she had to defend herself with the only tool she had: her teeth. Seeing my dog so stressed by living in a world that never gave her space or freedom, it became clear how much pressure we put on our urban dogs: they are expected to walk calmly on short leashes and ignore everything out of reach, to remain quiet when left home alone for long periods, and to tolerate frequent interruptions by doorbells, sirens, and delivery people. We're asking a lot of our dogs to live by our crazy human rules.

The good news is that both you and your dog can live together peacefully amid the chaos of a city, and it doesn't take as much effort as you might think. You don't need to quit your job to train your dog full-time (but wouldn't that be nice!), and your dog doesn't need to be able to balance an upright broom on his snout or jump through hoops of fire. In reality, by building clear communication with your dog and teaching him a handful of useful, straightforward behaviors, you can show your dog how to behave in ways that are polite to humans as well as rewarding for him. At the very least, this will require you to make some minor adjustments to your routine; at most, it will involve practicing and perfecting a few key training behaviors and learning how to apply these behaviors to various indoor and outdoor situations, all of which are outlined in the chapters that follow.

I know you're busy, so in true Brooklyn style, this book gets right to the point. It will address the most common dog behavior problems that urban owners face and provide practical solutions to getting a polite dog both indoors and out. Chapters 1 and 2 lay the foundation for training. Starting with Chapter 3, you can read the chapters in any order, depending on what your most urgent need is. Rather than give you a broad list of tricks and commands that you might never use, *BKLN Manners*™ focuses on fully developing a few polite behaviors and giving clear instructions for applying these behaviors to a variety of real-life situations. Nevertheless, if you'd like to learn additional city-friendly behaviors, such as Heel through intersections, Sit-Stays at crosswalks, Recalls at the park, or Drop Its for garbage on the sidewalk, you'll find the steps for these cues outlined in Chapter 7.

While all training takes time, commitment, and consistency, I will provide you with training solutions that can be smoothly integrated into your regular routine. In many cases, it doesn't take any extra time at all because you can train while you're already walking or spending time with your pup. The book is organized so that you can identify the problem you're having and then read through the different strategies to help. You'll notice that each chapter has multiple management and training strategies to modify your dog's behavior issue. See which strategies fit your lifestyle best. It is more effective to practice one strategy thoroughly than to superficially try many different ones. Dog training is not a one-size-fits-all endeavor; it is a unique experience based on your needs. If I see three clients in a row who all need help with leash walking, it's possible I will use a different strategy for each, depending on the dog's temperament, the owner's patience and interest in training, the external environment, and other factors.

This book covers four main areas of dog behavior that we consider problematic, with one chapter devoted to each:

B **Barking**

K **Knocking People Over**

L **Leash-Walking Problems**

N **Naughty When Alone**

Within these chapters are more specific problem-and-solution sections. You'll find that there is some overlap; for instance, a dog who jumps on passersby while walking with you on leash falls into both the K and L chapters. You'll also find that there is more than one problem in each chapter because, as you may have experienced, a dog can bark in more than one circumstance or may have more than one undesirable behavior while walking on leash. When you are ready to start training, check out the Appendix, which includes charts to track your progress.

And what about Pogo the Goldendoodle? I worked with his family for several sessions in their home, where he learned the foundation of being polite as outlined in Chapter 2. Later, he was one of the first graduates of my *BKLN Manners*™ group class. For walks, Pogo's family has learned how to teach Pogo polite behaviors, like sitting, rather than jumping on people, and when they know he is too excited to sit, they apply pain-free management strategies instead. Now, instead of mauling incoming guests with love, Pogo either takes a break in the bedroom while guests enter, or he sits politely on his mat until he is released. His home-alone freak-outs have been reduced from constant screams to a few whimpers now that he is getting the exercise and stimulation he needs. Walks are just that: walks. Pogo's acrobatics have subsided, and his humans have the tools to divert him from the sidewalk garbage buffet.

Is he a perfectly mannered gentleman all the time? Of course not! He's a dog, and still a young one at that. The last time I spoke to Pogo's family, I reminded them that training isn't really about what the dog does but about how the human reacts. Even the most well-behaved dog will do things that humans find undesirable. Fortunately, with some time and practice, we owners can learn how to prevent these rude doggie behaviors from happening. Pogo's family has learned how to address Pogo's doggie needs in a way that fits their busy urban lifestyle, and, as a result, everyone in the family is more at ease and learning together.

1

THINK
POSITIVE

The key to good doggie manners is preventing bad ones rather than doing damage control once the dog has already made a mistake. With every jump on a horrified houseguest, your dog will be reminded how much fun it is to jump on people, especially when—oh, goodie!—they squeal and thrash like squeaky toys. The habit becomes increasingly difficult to break because it is inherently enjoyable for your dog. Instead of struggling to calm down a dog who is already jumping wildly, prevent this habit from starting. If you know guests will be arriving at 4:00 p.m., get your dog happily in his crate or confined to your bedroom with a treat-stuffed toy by 3:55. Don't wait for the doorbell to ring and his doggie brain to explode.

As I mentioned in the Introduction, dog training actually has little to do with your dog. It has everything to do with how you react to your dog's behavior. My clients at Doggie Academy often assume that my own dogs are perfectly behaved at all times, as if they're finely tuned robots just awaiting my instructions. These owners sometimes gasp when I reveal, "No, no, trainers' dogs misbehave all the time!" Go to any obedience competition or other dog sport, which is full of professional trainers, and you will see dogs with behavior issues such as reactivity to other dogs, excessive barking, and overexcitement. Trainers simply know how to nip those issues in the bud. For example, in the case of excitement barking, a trainer will be in tune to her dog's emotions, able to pick up on the dog's subtle signs of excitement that come before the barking starts, and thus able to prevent the barking before it happens. If the dog has already barked, a trainer will immediately address it by asking the dog to perform a calm behavior to change his focus, thereby stopping the barking without force. You will never see a good trainer let a dog get completely out of control and only then try to correct the behavior. By following the steps in this book, you can channel your inner dog trainer to help your dog engage in polite, rather than rude, behaviors.

When following any given training strategy in this book, there will be several steps. Follow each step in order, and resist the temptation to skip steps. Often when dogs don't behave as we'd like, it's because we've pushed ahead too quickly and they're confused about what we're asking them. When training, you and your dog are learning a language together, so it's vital to take

baby steps forward and make sure you're communicating clearly at each step. If you've ever taken a language class in school, you know what happens if you skip a few lessons and then try to catch up. You're totally lost, and now your instructor is speaking indecipherable gibberish reminiscent of the adults in Peanuts cartoons. At this point, you're so stressed and confused that learning the language is pretty much impossible. As you train your dog, think of yourself as a language teacher who ensures that the student fully understands Lesson 1 before proceeding to Lesson 2. Go step by step with your training, and if your dog struggles at any point, revisit the previous step as outlined in the instructions.

TO TREAT OR NOT TO TREAT?

Most of us don't work for free. Because we know our company will pay us, we do all kinds of things we wouldn't otherwise do: wake up before sunrise, smile at coworkers before we've had our coffee, wear a uniform, and the list goes on. If we knew our company wouldn't pay us for our efforts, I'm sure most of us would quit—or at least slack off. So why is it that we think our dogs should work for free? For dogs, rewards, such as treats, are payment for a job well done, and you're the boss who has the ability to dish out those rewards. So be a good boss and pay your dog well, especially for difficult tasks like sitting when he'd much rather be jumping. This is the philosophy behind positive training, the form of training that I advocate because it is backed by extensive scientific research and has been proven to improve your dog's behavior in a way that is enjoyable for both of you.

Ask yourself, "What motivates my dog?" For most dogs, tiny pieces of training treats (including bits of "real food," like chicken, hot dog, or cheese) are highly motivating and easy to dispense. It is true that some dogs will gladly work for the reward of a "Good boy" and a pat on the head—and that's great! But if your dog doesn't fall into that category, be prepared to pay him in a currency that motivates him.

At the early stages of training, rewards accelerate the learning process because the dog gets excited to train with you and thinks, *Last time I put my rear on the ground, I got a cookie. I'm going to try that again!* The harder the task, the better your reward should be. There are generally two scenarios that make a task "hard" for the dog:

1. You are teaching him to do a new behavior. This could be something entirely new, like teaching him to lie down for the first time, or it could be a more difficult level of a behavior he already knows, such as a Stay for ten seconds when you've only practiced five-second Stays before. Your dog is working really hard here, and a super-tasty reward (or *high-value* reward, as trainers call it) will keep him in the game.

2. You are asking him to do something in a new or distracting environment. Asking your dog to sit in your living room is one thing; asking him to sit at a crosswalk in Times Square is another. When your dog is in a new, stressful, or distracting place, be ready to reward him handsomely for listening to you.

It's easy for dog owners to underestimate how hard their dogs are working to be polite, especially when being asked not to jump, not to bark, or not to pull on the leash. Granted, it doesn't look terribly impressive when a dog is sitting politely at a crosswalk, but think of it from the dog's perspective: he is surrounded by interesting smells, tasty-looking food wrappers, noisy vehicles, and other dogs and people. Asking him to sit in that situation is asking him simultaneously to not do about ten other things that he'd rather be doing, and that's very hard work. Therefore, in the early stages of training, the reward needs to be sufficiently motivating to keep him "in the game" with you.

I regularly see clients who believe that their dogs are not interested in treats, and while this is occasionally true, most of the time it's that the owners are asking their dogs to do something very difficult (such as sit in the presence of distractions) but not paying them adequately for it. When I teach a dog how to do a Sit-Stay indoors, I generally use a low-value treat, like kibble. When I teach the same dog the same Sit-Stay at a crosswalk, I upgrade to hot dogs because I'm asking the dog to pay attention to me and ignore all the excitement around him, which is no small task. Once the dog has gained more impulse control and can more easily do the Sit-Stay at the crosswalk, I can reduce the frequency and tastiness of my rewards.

Occasionally, your dog deserves a "jackpot"—a series of several treats in a row to reward a really great response or the completion of a difficult behavior. While dogs don't seem to notice the difference between a large treat and a small treat, they definitely know the difference between one treat and a series of treats. Being rewarded with a jackpot is like getting an A+ on an extra-difficult exam; you're left with a glow because your hard work was well worth it, and you feel more motivated for your next task.

Beyond treats, there are other rewards you can incorporate into your routine:

• After your dog comes to you when called, reward him by tossing a toy or briefly playing tug. *What fun it is to come to my human! I hope she asks me to come again*, he thinks.

• Give the dog his meal only if he sits while you put the bowl on the floor. You were going to feed him anyway, so why not ask him to be polite for his dinner?

• Have him sit or lie down before being allowed on the sofa or bed. I usually have no problem with allowing my dogs on the couch with me, but they have to ask "Please" by sitting or lying down to get invited up.

• Only put on the leash if your dog is sitting. Here, the opportunity to get leashed up is the reward.

• Only let the dog out the door if he sits and waits until you say a release word, such as "OK."

These kinds of "life rewards" accelerate your dog's manners training because he is learning to be polite for whatever he wants throughout the day. Sitting is a behavior that doesn't just

get him a cookie during training sessions, it also gets him whatever he wants in his regular routine. With consistency, he learns that whenever he wants something, he should sit quietly. And then you'll find him offering the Sit whenever he wants something, without even being asked. Good dog!

This rewards-based style of training might be different from what you grew up with or even at odds with what some trainers in your area are promoting. The problem with the older, largely outdated "dominance" style of training is that it often relies on pain- and fear-inducing tactics to compel a dog to behave. While advocates of that method might say that they are teaching dogs to "respect" their owners, I am not convinced that dogs have the capacity for respect; respect is a loaded word that describes a rather complex relationship between two individuals. It is widely accepted that dogs have basic emotions such as fear, happiness, anger, and anxiety; however, it has not been proven that dogs have complex emotions that require reflection, including guilt and respect.

Sitting and waiting for the "OK" to eat.

Books about dog cognition and behavior, such as *Dog Sense* by John Bradshaw, have gone in-depth into this topic using recent research. Those trainers who demand that dogs respect them may at times resort to techniques that are simply hurting or scaring the dogs. *If my dog doesn't sit, I pop him with the choke chain, and he sits to have that pain relieved.* Yes, it works, but is that because the dog respects his owner as his leader? Or simply because he wants that pain to stop? This kind of training can easily be misused, eroding the trust between you and your dog and making your dog defensive around you. Training should not be a battle of wills or a struggle to be on top because it puts you at odds with your dog, and, as a result, nobody wins. Rather, training should be fun and simple enough for anyone, kids included, to do without the risk of hurting or scaring a dog. It should be something you and your dog do together.

Positive training techniques, on the other hand, are proven to be very effective in teaching polite behaviors, with the added benefit of building clear communication and a lifelong bond with your dog. With positive training, when the dog doesn't sit (or lie down or stay) as you've asked, rather than punish him, you simply withhold the reward, which is "punishment" enough to a dog. Then ask yourself why he didn't sit. Did you use a different tone of voice this time? Were you standing farther away from him? Did the phone ring at the same time, distracting your dog? In all of these cases, it's not the dog's fault that he didn't sit. It's the human's mistake for either asking the dog to sit in a way he didn't understand or asking the dog to sit it in a context in which it is currently too difficult for him to concentrate. When the focus is on clear communication rather than dominance, you and your dog can learn as a team.

MANAGEMENT VERSUS TRAINING

Let's say your dog jumps on the sofa without permission, and you'd like him to stop. What should you do? Well, the answer depends on several factors, ranging from the amount of time you have to train to the layout of your home.

Management is generally the easiest option, as it doesn't require actual training. Essentially, when you manage the space around you, you create an environment in which the dog can't engage in the bad behavior. For example, if you don't want your dog jumping on your sofa while you're out, lay a folding chair across it. Now the sofa isn't soft anymore, and your dog won't be interested in lying there. Don't have a folding chair? You can also manage the space by blocking his access to that room: shut certain doors, use a baby gate, or put him in a crate. Management is the appropriate choice when you can't dedicate time to training or when you're not there to monitor your dog (because you can't train if you're not present).

Though management is generally easier to implement than training, it doesn't actually teach the dog to be more polite. You are simply preventing the undesired behavior from happening by blocking the dog's access to whatever is causing the problem. When the sofa is unprotected, your pup will likely hop back on it. There is nothing wrong with the management approach, as long as you realize its limitations.

Training, on the other hand, is when we teach our dogs to do a polite behavior instead of the bad one. While I don't have a problem gently telling a dog "No," it's necessary to follow it up by telling him what to do instead. This, of course, takes some time to practice. In the case of jumping on the sofa, one simple training strategy is to teach the dog to sit before being invited onto the sofa. By sitting and asking "Please," he can have the reward of the sofa. Additionally, I would teach him a cue to go to his doggie bed because there are times when I don't want the dog on the sofa, regardless of how politely he asks. Notice that by telling him to go to his own bed, I'm not just saying "No" to the sofa but also giving him instructions on where to go instead. Training is the way to have a truly polite dog, because it teaches your dog life skills that allow him to interact peacefully with you, your family, and your friends.

Imagine that your dog has learned how to jump up on your kitchen counter and help himself to anything and everything in your cupboards. What would you do? The management strategy is to block the dog's access to this area. Close doors, use gates (open floor plans be damned!), use child safety locks to protect the cupboards, or crate your dog. All of these measures will prevent the problem behavior, but it may not actually train the dog to stay off the counters.

For a dog who is accustomed to his crate, the crate can be a helpful management tool.

What's It Worth to Ya?

When Doggie Academy clients bring their dogs to group classes, we ask them to pack several levels of rewards. Just because your dog will work for pieces of his dry food at home, it might be unrealistic to think that kibble will hold his attention in a bustling group class with constant distractions.

In addition, certain behaviors might warrant higher level rewards. If your dog is especially bouncy, for example, be ready to reward him with the highest value rewards when he practices self-control, as in the stay or heel cues. Here are some examples of low-, mid-, and high-value treats:

Low-value: Pieces of dry dog food, dry treats, bits of carrots, a rope toy
Mid-value: Soft and stinky training treats, a squeaky toy
High-value: Bits of chicken, cheese, deli meat, or hot dogs; throwing a ball

What about training your dog to stop counter-surfing? You can certainly do this, but just remember that every "No" should be followed with a "Do this instead." Two of the strategies explained in later chapters would apply. One option is to teach a Leave It cue, which instructs your dog to walk away from the counter. Leave It basically tells the dog, "Stop approaching that tempting place and walk away instead." Another possibility is teaching the dog that the kitchen is off-limits (but remember that you can only enforce such a rule when you're home). When you're in the kitchen cooking something delicious, send your dog out of the room and have him lie down on his bed or mat, which you can place right outside the kitchen. This is a variation of Place from Chapter 3, which tells the dog to go relax on his bed rather than to sniff around, looking for trouble. For counter-surfing or any other number of problems, such as begging at the table or dashing out an open door, Place prevents the problem from happening. Prevention is always a better strategy than doing damage control once the dog has already stolen your Thanksgiving turkey from the counter or run out the door as you were signing for your package.

In many cases, a combination of training and management strategies is often the best approach, using management to ensure that the bad habit doesn't continue when you're not home. Even when you are home, management stops the unwanted behavior from occurring; during that time, you can train your dog to behave differently in the presence of his triggers, whether it's food on the counter or a squirrel crossing your path during walks.

SEQUENCE FOR TRAINING

When it comes to communication between you and your dog, it's a little different from the kinds of communication we're used to. (However, the positive training techniques we use to train our dogs can also be used to train spouses or kids! Karen Pryor explains how to use positive reinforcement with animals and humans alike in her classic book *Don't Shoot the Dog*.) When teaching your dog to lie down, for instance, what you do after the dog lies down is far more important than what you did before he lay down. What that means is that your cue to lie down doesn't teach him much; it's by "marking" and "rewarding" the correct Down position that you are actually teaching him. This is the typical sequence for teaching a dog a brand-new behavior:

There are several strategies to replace counter-surfing with acceptable behavior.

Cue Princess to lie down. At first, you may need to lure her into position with a treat so she can follow the scent downward. Princess lies down.

Mark it. The moment Princess is fully lying down, say "Yes!" Why? "Yes" is a word that we generally don't use around our dogs otherwise, so the dog will make a clear connection that the word "yes" means "good job; a reward is coming." You may also click with a clicker (see page 24) or use a different verbal marker, such as "Good dog!" (If you want to get technical, trainers tend to avoid "Good dog/boy/girl" because we also tend to use it when Princess is simply being cute or funny, but we rarely say "Yes" to a dog in other situations.) The word itself is not so important, as long as you use the same word every time and say it at the exact moment the dog does the desired behavior. Marking the desired behavior is the way Princess learns what we want her to do.

Reward it. In the early stages of learning, rewards serve to encourage the dog to try the behavior again. It was so rewarding the first time, why not lie down next time, too?

Marking and rewarding go hand in hand. Marking identifies the behavior we want, and rewarding encourages the dog to do it again. If you mark too slowly—for instance, after Princess has popped back up from the Down—there is the chance that you're marking the wrong behavior, and she will learn that "Down" means "lie down and stand up quickly" rather than "lie down and stay down." Rewards should come pretty quickly after the verbal marker, within a second or two of marking, especially when you're teaching a new behavior. Always reward Princess while she's still doing the desired behavior. In this case, reward her while she's lying down so she learns how awesome it is to lie down.

If Princess starts to lie down but then pops up into a stand, we mark that moment, too. We use a no-reward marker (NRM) like "Oops" or "Uh-uh" to identify the moment the dog did the wrong thing. When that happens, just say your NRM and start over. There's no need for an angry tone, and, please, no physical corrections. When the dog makes a mistake, it is just that: a mistake. Imagine if your teacher punished you every time you made a mistake; you probably wouldn't want to learn from this person anymore, and rightly so!

The last handy word is a release word, telling Princess that she can stop lying down now. I use "OK." Without this word, she won't know for how long to lie there, and she will eventually get up on her own. It's better for you so release with "OK" before that happens.

CUES

When I was growing up, dogs went to "obedience school" and obeyed "commands." The attitude toward the dog was, "Do it. And if you don't, expect unpleasant consequences." As times have changed and training has evolved, so has the lingo. *Obedience* and *commands* are out, and *manners* and *cues* are in. This shows the current direction of dog training, which is more about the dog being polite than being obedient, and we recognize that the dog certainly has a choice whether to obey our cues or not. The goal of positive dog training is to make the polite behavior—such as sitting, rather than jumping, to be petted by a stranger—the better choice in the dog's mind. Sure, he can choose to be rude, but only being polite gets him what he wants, so it's in his best interest to listen to your cue.

Cues reveal a great deal about the differences between humans and dogs. We humans talk a lot, and it's quite a challenge to get us to stop. In *BKLN Manners*™ and other group classes I teach, I always remind participants to say the cue only once. And almost every participant breaks this rule again and again, not because they are bad at following instructions but because they are normal human beings who tend to repeat the same thing, louder and louder, until they are acknowledged. (For an enlightening comparison of human and dog behavior, I recommend Patricia McConnell's *The Other End of the Leash*.) If you think about dogs, though, they generally don't vocalize, excluding arousing or alarming events like a doorbell ringing or rowdy off-leash play. In general, their world is pretty quiet, and for us to train them effectively, we need to put our human tendencies aside and follow suit.

So, from now on, unless told otherwise, give the cue only once. Once! (There I go, repeating myself like a human.) Imagine if you say, "Sadie, sit. Sit. SIT!" Finally, she does, but what has the cue become? It's become two cues that Sadie can ignore, and only the third time does she have to listen. Instead, say the cue once and then ensure that the dog is in a situation in which she will definitely sit. This will be outlined in the steps of later chapters.

If, while training something new, you say the cue (e.g, "Sit) and the dog doesn't immediately respond, count to ten in your head. Dogs, especially puppies, take a little extra time to process what you've said. Give your dog the chance to respond to your first cue; most dogs do if you

The Clicker Conundrum

The clicker makes a sound that "marks" the desirable behavior.

I'm frequently asked, "Do I need a clicker to train my dog?" The answer, for better or worse, is, "It depends." A clicker simply provides a clear way to mark a dog's correct behavior; that is, you click the moment the dog does what you're asking. If you're teaching your dog to give you his paw, you would click the moment his paw touches your hand.

In theory, it is no different from saying "Yes" to mark the correct behavior, but clickers have certain advantages:

- A clicker provides a unique, consistent sound. This gives the dog very clear feedback, compared to your voice, which fluctuates. (Think of all the different ways you could say "Yes!")
- Some owners have better timing with clickers than their voices.
- The clicking sound can motivate dogs to work harder, and it can help some to focus on the task. It's as if the dog gets excited to win more "clicks."
- Because of the reasons above, clicker training is useful for shaping difficult behaviors by breaking them down into smaller steps. For example, if teaching a high five, you could first click a little paw lift, then a slightly higher paw lift, and so on.

Clickers also have some disadvantages:

- You have one more tool to hold. While there are many variations, including ones that slip on your finger like a ring, you're still carrying one more piece of equipment.
- Some dogs are afraid of the clicking sound. This doesn't mean you can't clicker train, but you might need to purchase a quiet clicker or condition the dog to muffled clicking sounds at first.
- Poor clicker timing can be more confusing for the dog than an ill-timed verbal marker. Occasionally an owner needs to practice clicker timing before introducing it to a dog.
- Some kids can't keep their hands off of the clicker. There is no point in using a clicker if a family member routinely uses it for anything other than training.
- Once your dog fully understands how to, say, high five, you no longer need the clicker. Determining when to stop clicking for a certain behavior can be confusing for some people.

Ultimately, the choice is yours. I tend to use clickers with Doggie Academy clients who are interested in the training process or who plan to do higher level activities such as trick training or freestyle (described in Chapter ⑧). I also often use clicker training with distractible or reactive dogs because the sound is clearer than a verbal marker, which makes training a little easier and faster.

just give them sufficient time. If you completely lose his attention, or more than ten seconds has passed, then reevaluate what may have gone wrong and start over. The next time you ask for a Sit, create a situation in which you know he will sit, possibly by moving to a quieter area or using a tastier treat, so he can be successful with just one cue.

FOUR-FOR-FOUR

Let's go back to the metaphor of taking a language class. Either as a child or an adult, you have probably learned a foreign language to some extent. In my case, I have been taking Japanese language classes for more than a decade so I can communicate better with my Japanese in-laws. One program I took was divided into twelve levels, but there was no exam at the end of each level to determine if the students really understood the material enough to move on to the next level. All of the students moved up to more difficult levels at the end of each semester, regardless of proficiency. Without an assessment to gauge each student's comprehension, what happened was, by Level 5 or so, students started getting in over their heads, lost their motivation, and many ultimately dropped out. Having a background in education, I already knew that when the material got overwhelming, I would need to repeat a level. And I did, at Level 6 and then again at Level 10. Despite criticism from my classmates ("Why are you wasting your money to repeat old material?" "If you want to feel like the best student in the class, maybe you should retake Level 1, ha ha!"), it was repeating those levels that allowed me to really absorb the information I'd learned and smoothly progress to Level 12—while my snarky classmates gave up and dropped out, one by one.

The same concept holds true for dogs. When teaching a new behavior, we want to make sure that the dog fully understands the criteria for Level 1 before we move on to Level 2. I recommend practicing "four-for-four," which involves working on a new behavior at Level 1 until you get it correct four times in a row. It might take only your first four responses to move up to the next level, or it might take several more repetitions until you can get four correct responses in a row. Regardless, four-for-four will tell you that your dog really gets it, at which point you can proceed to Level 2 and practice at that level until you get four correct responses in a row. This is how you prevent yourself from pushing the dog too far too fast, which would put him under the same stress as a Japanese language student who can't keep up.

To illustrate, if you're practicing Place with Distance from Chapter 3, which teaches the dog to go to his bed and remain there, you would start by getting four-for-four while you stand next to the bed. This means repeating the same cue from the same short distance as many times as needed until your dog correctly goes to his bed four times in a row. Once you have those four correct responses, take one small sidestep away from the bed and cue the dog to his "place." Now you're at a more difficult level because you're farther from the bed, so you'll need to practice at this distance as many times as needed until your dog gets four correct responses in a row. Once you have four-for-four at that distance, take another small step away, get another four-for-four, and so forth.

Four-for-four is intended to prevent you, the handler, from advancing levels too quickly, and it works well for the majority of dogs. I should mention, though, that not all dogs require four-for-four to achieve success at a particular level. In fact, a few dogs may actually get bored by the second or third correct response, and if the difficulty doesn't increase, they will lose focus. It's fine to modify your training plan for a dog who only needs two-for-two or three-for-three.

The purpose of four-for-four is that you will never push your dog beyond his limits. Still, you might reach a point where, after practicing several sequences of a ten-step Heel, it becomes clear that your dog simply cannot get four-for-four correct. If this happens, it's time to either lower the criteria or take a break, depending on how you and your dog are feeling. For dogs and humans alike, it's frustrating to be asked to perform a task again and again without success. If your dog's head is still in the game, do one five-step Heel and call it quits for a few hours. If you think even a five-step Heel is asking too much, just take a break immediately. Your dog's success at Heel will be the product of repeated practice sessions over several weeks, so there is no need to push it when your dog's brain is already fried on one particular day.

DISTRACTIONS

The most successful trainers, whether amateur or professional, are the ones who can leave their frustrations aside while training. Imagine if your third-grade teacher huffed and puffed every time you misspelled a word. Would it make you learn to spell any faster? When a dog misbehaves or doesn't follow your cue, it's never personal. Generally, the dog either does not understand your cue (perhaps because you didn't do four-for-four), or you are in a situation with excessive distractions. Both of these situations can be easily remedied with methodical training.

Always set your dog up for success when teaching a new behavior. Start training new things in a setting with no distractions, such as in a quiet room. I consider this the preschool level for your dog, because it should be like a game: easy and fun. As your dog is successful at each level, he can move up a "grade," which means you can gradually increase the level of distractions while training. For instance, when I teach a dog polite leash walking, the progress looks something like this:

1. Preschool: Start inside your home and use lots of treats to reward polite walking until the dog really understands it.
2. Kindergarten: Still indoors, gradually reduce the number of treat rewards.
3. Elementary school: Go to a low-distraction outdoor area (a backyard or side street at the most quiet time of day) and use lots of treats to reward polite walking until the dog really understands it.
4. Middle school: Still in a low-distraction outdoor area, gradually reduce the number of treat rewards.
5. Junior high: Go to a somewhat higher distraction outdoor area, like a side street at a busy time, and use lots of treats to reward polite walking until the dog really understands it.

Gradually increase the distractions until you reach PhD level, which might be a train station or bustling urban area. You'll find that, even though you're starting from scratch by using more treats for each new level of distraction, your dog will be able to progress quickly. By working up to higher distractions methodically, you'll never overwhelm your dog. In the process, you'll also fine-tune your communication and enhance your bond with him. Therefore, training actually goes much faster when you stick to the plan and avoid skipping steps because your dog "gets it" and has fun each step of the way.

HOW TO FIND A TRAINER

In the subsequent chapters, I will provide suggestions for when to contact a trainer rather than try to work through your dog's issue yourself. There are many excellent dog trainers out there, but because dog training is an unregulated profession in which anyone can call him- or herself a trainer, you need to choose carefully. Personally, I'm big on certifications because they show a professional's commitment to the field and willingness to participate in the continuing-education requirements that are required to maintain certification. But not all certificates are created equal.

There are few things to look for to ensure that a trainer is trustworthy and qualified. If you see CPDT-KA or CPDT-KSA after the trainer's name, you can feel comfortable knowing that the trainer has passed a third-party assessment test that focuses on scientifically proven models of training. Failing that, find out if a trainer has graduated from a dog-training school or apprenticeship program; the trainer should mention this information on his or her website or provide it upon request. But, again, because dog training is unregulated, some programs are excellent and others are not. Research the program to see its philosophy, which should

It's common for a dog to be distracted by the sights, sounds, and smells of the city.

Acronyms Explained

CCPDT: Certification Council for Professional Dog Trainers
APDT: Association of Professional Dog Trainers
CAAB: Certified Applied Animal Behaviorist
ACAAB: Associate Certified Applied Animal Behaviorist
DACVB: Diplomate of American College of Veterinary Behaviorists
IAABC: International Association of Animal Behavior Consultants
CDBC: Certified Dog Behavior Consultant
CBCC: Certified Behavior Consultant Canine
CABC: Certified Animal Behavior Consultant

emphasize positive training (also called *force-free* or *rewards-based* training). Be wary of trainers or schools that frequently use words like *alpha*, *dominance*, or *wolf pack*, because these terms indicate an outdated and inaccurate understanding of dog behavior. Lastly, a trainer's membership in associations such as the Association of Professional Dog Trainers (APDT) or a dog-sport association is a plus, but just be aware that these organizations do not evaluate trainers' qualifications. That being said, if you see that a trainer holds a leadership position in any association, or participates in canine sports, or volunteers in animal rescue, it usually indicates an individual who sees dogs not just as a job but as a passion.

The most difficult behavior problems often fall to behaviorists, who have the highest qualifications and are harder to find than trainers, depending on your area. If someone calls him- or herself a behaviorist, look for credentials. Technically, the term behaviorist refers to applied animal behaviorists (look for CAAB or ACAAB) or veterinary *behaviorists* (DACVB); these are professionals with advanced academic degrees. Other acronyms that indicate experienced behavior consultants include IAABC, CDBC, CBCC, and CABC. If a professional claims to be a behaviorist, he or she should have some kind of certification to back it up.

It's also worth noting that seemingly everyone—your neighbors, your vet, your groomer, complete strangers—fancy themselves experts on dog training. Please ignore every single one of them. Yes, even your vet, unless he or she has been formally trained in behavior. (Surprisingly, vets generally do not take coursework in animal behavior.) You wouldn't want me, a trainer, diagnosing your dog's illness, right? And you certainly wouldn't want to leave me with a pair of scissors and your hairy pooch for the day! So for all things doggie, please only take advice from trained and trusted professionals in that specific field.

LET'S GET THIS PARTY STARTED

It's time to get training! Before you start, keep a few things in mind.

Tip 1: Training is a time to put your emotions aside. If you've had a terrible day and your last nerve is about to snap, the training can wait. Likewise, if you find yourself or your dog getting frustrated in the middle of a training session, it's time for a break. I'd suggest short training sessions of five minutes or less, especially for young dogs. Additionally, always begin and end on a positive note. To do this, I warm up by beginning each training session with something the dog already knows. For instance, if my goal for a training session is a ten-second Stay, I will warm up with a regular old Sit, which the dog already knows. Then, when I'm ready to end the training session, I have two options: (1) I can practice until my dog achieves four-for-four at a new level, like a perfect Stay at ten seconds. This assumes that both our heads are still fully in the game and neither of us feels frustrated. (2) If one of us is showing early signs of struggling, I'll make my last cue an easy one so the dog will definitely be able to do it correctly. For example, if my dog is getting frustrated and making mistakes with a ten-second Stay, I'll reduce it to five seconds, get a good response, and end there. If you can't get a good response at the easier level, don't push it. Take a break. Just ask yourself, "Why did my dog (or I) feel so frustrated?" and aim to avoid putting yourselves in that situation in the future.

Tip 2: Use four-for-four when training to ensure that your dog truly understands each step. I also recommend documenting your progress in (see Appendix) by noting exactly where you leave off in each training session. Imagine if you don't record your progress. "Was it a Place with 1 foot or 2 feet of distance between me and the dog's mat?" To avoid that kind of confusion, record the highest level of training you achieved each session, such as, "Place with 18 inches between me and the mat." Then, when you start your next session, you can warm up with an easier Place, at 1 foot away, and then increase to greater distances. Be methodical in your training, and you'll reap the rewards for your dog's entire life.

Tip 3: Real-life training takes time, and all dogs learn at their own pace. We're often inspired by dog-training television shows, thrilling agility events, or incredible musical freestyle routines, but these things can also dishearten us when we look at our own dogs. Just remember that behind every success story are countless hours of hard work, complete with setbacks and frustration, breakthroughs and joy. Even the most incredible doggie stars had to start by learning not to jump, not to pull on the leash, and not to destroy the furniture. So my advice is to meet your dog where he is, even if it seems like you're not making progress as quickly as you'd like.

It can feel frustrating when you think your dog "should" know a certain behavior by now, and it's easy to blame the dog and assume that he is an evil genius who is playing mind games with you. In reality, your dog is failing to do what you're asking because he truly does not yet understand how to perform that behavior in that environment. Many owners tell me, "My dog knows how to sit, but he refuses to do it outside." In fact, the dog may have learned how to sit inside the home, but he doesn't have a clue that the Sit cue means "sit" outdoors, too. He's not playing tricks, he simply hasn't been taught that "Sit" applies to all environments, including outdoors. The chapters that follow will show you how to teach polite behaviors so that your dog *generalizes* them, which means that he understands the cue in all situations. Great dogs are made, not born, and regardless of your dog's size, age, or breed, he can learn to be a polite member of your family.

...aaaand Action!

It often helps to see certain training strategies in action. Visit bklnmanners.com to find additional descriptions and instructional videos to augment some of the management and training techniques in the following chapters.

TRAINING: FIRST THINGS FIRST

Almost every day, I walk past a hapless dog owner, yelling at her dog to "Sit, sit, sit!" at the crosswalk, while her oblivious dog is completely focused on an overweight city squirrel up ahead. Frustration building, the owner pushes the dog's rear end down, which only causes the dog to squirm away from the pressure. Eventually, the owner either gives up or starts to get physical. But the truth is, the attempt to train here was dead before it even started. Why? Because the owner never got her dog's attention before asking for the Sit behavior.

Often we ask our dogs to do things, particularly to sit or to come, when their attention is consumed by something else, making this an unfair request. If you're engrossed in playing a video game, and your roommate asks you to clean the kitchen, you might not even hear her request. But if your roommate asks you while your attention is fully on her, you'll surely respond. (Whether you'll actually clean the kitchen is another matter.) Likewise, when training a dog, it's important to get his attention first and then ask him to perform a behavior.

BUT FIRST, EYE CONTACT

It's no wonder our dogs have trouble paying attention to us, especially outdoors. The urban world is a highly distracting place for your dog: squirrels hopping, other dogs approaching, ambulance sirens blaring, and the delicious contents of ripped garbage bags beckoning. It's likely your dog doesn't even know you're there on the walk with him. But once he learns that it's rewarding to look at you, even when distractions are present, you can control him in all situations. That's all you need: a look. Having a well-behaved dog isn't about how many tricks he can do or how many cues he knows, but rather how well he can pay attention to you in any environment. Once your dog learns to look at you, you can prevent him from lunging at, chasing, or barking at distractions simply by asking for his attention and, when you have it, by cuing him to do something polite. But without getting his attention first, you won't be able to ask for the polite behavior.

As humans, we've got the upper hand because we control the resources dogs want: meals, treats, toys, the leash, the door, and so on. Use those resources to your advantage. In my home, if my dog Batman wants me to throw a toy for him, he's got to look at me first. Not jump up. Not bark. Not stare at the toy. All of those things get him nowhere, and I simply stand like a statue while he flails about. I don't give him a cue to sit or move my body to get his attention; rather, I quietly wait. The moment he looks me in the eye, bingo! I toss the toy. It's a win-win: I got Batman's attention, and Batman got his toy.

This kind of training goes a long way in teaching my dog how to communicate with me because he learns that his actions will lead to certain consequences. When he barks and jumps for a toy, the consequence is that I completely ignore him. He'll think to himself, *Hmm, this doesn't seem to be working. Maybe I should try another strategy to get that toy.* That's when, ultimately, he's going to look at me. The consequence of his eye contact? Exactly what he wants: the toy! He's just learned, without me having to say anything, what kind of behavior (eye contact) gets him what he wants and what kind of behaviors (jumping and barking) aren't even worth trying because they yield nothing. I want him to think he's so clever—all he has to do is look at this silly human, and he gets his toy. He doesn't need to bark, jump, or spin around anymore, so those behaviors will be culled from his repertoire in the future. Go ahead, let him think to himself, *Humans are so easy to train. Just give them a look and I get what I want!*

CHECK ME OUT

Start the Check Me Out exercise in a quiet place with no distractions. There is no verbal cue, which is great practice for you, the human, to be a little more doglike. This exercise, when practiced consistently, will teach your dog that when he wants something, he should look at you in order to get it. Jumping, barking, and other rude behaviors won't get him what he wants.

In the beginning, our criteria are pretty low. The dog only has to quickly glance at your face in order to "win" his treat. It's critical to set the training session up so your dog can win the Check Me Out game easily. The more fun it is for him, the more quickly he'll learn. That's why it's best to start in a quiet location and initially reward him for even the slightest glance. Remember, you and your dog are on the same team, so when he wins, you also win by getting a better behaved dog.

How to Teach Check Me Out
1. Hold a treat in your outstretched hand. Say nothing but maintain gentle eye contact with your dog. Avoid leaning into your dog or staring wide-eyed. Be natural and relaxed.
2. Wait for the dog to look at you. He will likely look at the treat for a while first, or he might jump up or bark at you. Hold still and ignore all of these undesirable responses.
3. The moment he looks at your face, immediately mark it with "Yes!" and reward him with the treat from your hand. Revisit Chapter 1 if you're not sure how to mark and reward.
From there, practice this exercise at home, indoors, in different scenarios:
- Use a variety of treats.
- Use his food bowl. Require eye contact before you put the bowl down.
- Use toys. Hold a toy and wait for his eye contact before you initiate the tug or fetch game. Ignore any rude behavior to get the toy; only eye contact while being quiet will get him the toy.
- At walk time, open the door to go outside only after he looks at you.
- In order to be invited on the couch with you, he must look at you and get your permission to come up. When he looks at you, lean back and pat the couch to invite him up. If he tries to jump up without asking permission, gently block him with your forearm or body and wait for him to ask politely with eye contact. Note: This strategy only applies to times when you are already on the couch.

Then, practice Check Me Out when you're outside playing or walking. Increase the value of your treats to the really good stuff, like tiny pieces of boiled chicken, hot dog, or cheese, because you're asking your dog to work much harder in a new or distracting place. Even though he's already learned Check Me Out indoors, it doesn't mean he'll have a clue what it means outdoors. Here is a sample sequence.

◄ Ilyssa holds out a treat and says nothing. Susu looks at the treat and first tries her old standby trick: Give Paw. Ilyssa holds still while Susu then thinks about how to get that treat.

◄ Aha! The moment Susu looks at Ilyssa's face, Ilyssa marks it with "Yes"...

◄ ...and Susu gets the treat.

1. Practice Check Me Out with treats while you're standing on your stoop or in your yard. Get four-for-four. Practice at this level until your dog really grasps it, which could take several minutes—or several days.

2. Next, take a break from your walk on the sidewalk or in the park by practicing Check Me Out. Choose a place with few distractions, like a park bench that's off the main path, so your dog can focus on the game and be successful. Get four-four-four at this level. Continue to make time for a quick Check Me Out game during every walk.

3. Practice the game as before, but in a more crowded or noisy area. If your dog loses focus on the game, it likely means the distractions are too intense for him (or the rewards are not sufficiently motivating for this difficult task), and you should either move to a quieter spot or upgrade to super-tasty rewards, such as bits of meat.

4. Once you start playing Check Me Out outside, your dog, without prompting, might look up at you once in a while during your walks. If he does, reward the heck out of him. This means he is generalizing the behavior and considers any time to be training time. Your dog always has the choice to acknowledge you or ignore you, and if he looks up to check in with you at any time, it means he is choosing you over the squirrels and other distractions. Good dog!

See the Appendix for a sample plan and chart to help you track your progress when training Check Me Out.

Troubleshooting

Problem: My dog will only look at me when it's totally quiet.

Solution: Keep working in "easy" locations for several days, or longer, until he really gets it. While indoors, use as many different rewards as possible: treats, his food dish, toys, the leash, and access to any area he wants, such as the couch. Then, before attempting Check Me Out outside, add an intermediate step to help solidify the behavior. For this step, you'll practice for several days in the same quiet location, but you'll add a mild distraction. While practicing, add some background noise by playing recordings of traffic, dogs barking, or something similar, all of which can be easily found online. You can also add some activity to your indoor setting by asking family members to walk around in the background, rolling a ball behind you as you present your Check Me Out treat, or creating other movement in the training space.

Problem: My dog seems uncomfortable looking at me.

Solution: Some dogs naturally avoid eye contact, but there are ways to make these dogs more at ease. First, make sure your body is in a natural position and you're calmly looking at your dog during this exercise. If you're crouched over your dog or staring intensely at him, it's no wonder he feels uncomfortable! Provided that your body language is relaxed, you can use a technique called shaping, in which you reward the dog for any small step toward the end goal. At first, any time he glances away from the treat, in any direction, mark and reward. Get four-for-four. (Revisit Chapter 1 if you need to review four-for-four.) As the training sessions progress, tighten the criteria. Next time, mark and reward only glances in the general direction of your body. Get four-for-four. Next, mark and reward only glances anywhere on your body. Continue tightening the criteria so that you only mark and reward glances that are closer and closer to your face. Ultimately, only mark and reward when your dog looks into or near your eyes. Let your dog dictate how fast he progresses; it's better to go slowly and keep your dog comfortable than to set a goal like "Tucker must be giving me direct eye contact by Tuesday," which can backfire if Tucker gets overwhelmed from too much practice.

Problem: My dog will only briefly glance at me, and then he looks away.

Solution: In the beginning, this is fine. As with the previous problem, first make sure that your body language and eye contact is relaxed, so as not to make your dog uncomfortable. Then, you can shape a more prolonged eye contact. For the first few sessions, mark and reward any quick glance at your face. Get four-for-four. Once your dog is consistently glancing at you, tighten the criteria by only marking and rewarding glances that are a split second longer than before. Continue increasing the criteria until you are only marking and rewarding when your dog holds his eye contact for one second (or longer, if you want to keep going). Get four-for-four at each level to be sure you're not pushing the dog beyond his capabilities.

Problem: My dog constantly looks at me now. I'm always being watched!

Solution: So you've turned your dog into a bit of a stalker. This happened with Batman, who took to Check Me Out a little too readily and is capable of staring at me for a full ninety minutes before his dinnertime. (I must say, his strategy works—I never forget to feed him on time.) But just because your dog is politely getting your attention with eye contact in order to have his dinner, a walk, or couch access, it doesn't mean you always have to say "Yes" to his request. I have a response, "That's all," that tells my dogs that I will not comply with their request at this time. Let's be honest: sometimes I don't want to be covered in a pile of dogs while I sit on the couch, and I'm within my rights to tell the dogs "That's all" and send them to their beds instead. The key with this response is that you have to mean

it. After I say "That's all," I cut off all eye contact and ignore any further doggie requests for attention. There are numerous times when I've told them "That's all" and then regretted it, wishing I had invited them on the couch with me instead, but if I cave in and give them permission to come up after initially saying "No," then I'm only confusing them for the next time. Check out Chapter 3 for full details about implementing "That's all."

DOGS OF Ⓑ Ⓚ Ⓛ Ⓝ

Meet Susu

These soulful eyes belong to Susu, a three-year-old Pit Bull who was found as a stray and taken to Animal Care Center (the city shelter) in Harlem. She was lucky enough to be placed in a foster home with Pound Hounds Res-Q, where she met her doting new family, Joe and Ilyssa. Joe says, "Susu can do it all! She's an energetic Pit Bull who can move through an agility course just as much as she can snuggle on the sofa and stay inside on a rainy day. Susu, like so many Pit Bulls we have met, is a goofy, lovable, smart, and stubborn girl."

Susu loves pretty much everything, from car rides to hikes to other dogs. In fact, it's her unbridled enthusiasm for other dogs that became Susu's biggest training challenge, especially when on leash. Once she spotted an approaching dog, she found it hard to focus on anything else. Joe and Ilyssa have used a few of the strategies in Chapter ❺, starting with Emergency Recall, to teach Susu to focus on them rather than a passing dog. From there, they worked up to Hand Targeting in the presence of another dog. You can see photos of Susu's Hand Targeting skills in Chapter ❺.

B

BARKING

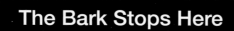

The Bark Stops Here

Asking why dogs bark is like asking why people talk. Just like humans who chat, yell, laugh, and cry, canines express a wide variety of doggie emotions through their vocalizations. As a result, there is no one solution to stopping all barking. In fact, the goal should never be to stop the dog from barking altogether, just as you'd never insist a person be completely silent her whole life. Rather, a realistic goal is to allow the dog to bark sufficiently to make his point—for example, two or three barks to alert the family that someone is at the door—and then let his human take it from there.

The ideal training strategy addresses the underlying emotion that causes the barking and then offers a calm alternative activity for the dog to engage in so he doesn't feel the need to bark so incessantly. (For a thorough description of the kinds of barking, I recommend the book *Barking: The Sound of a Language* by Turid Rugaas.) Dogs often engage in *alarm barking* when they are faced with potentially intrusive or threatening stimuli like doorbells, passersby outside the window, and unwanted guests, such as the postal worker. The dog is essentially warning anyone within earshot: "Hey, everybody, danger!" Of course, you know the postal worker is just there to drop off your mail, just like every other day, with no nefarious plans to break into your home. Nevertheless, if your dog is sounding his alarm, you need to address it as if the danger were real because, at that moment, it is very real to your dog. This means no yelling or punishing the dog; he is simply expressing his emotions, and his barking could actually alert you to a real danger someday.

Many city dwellers, myself included, like the added security of knowing the dog will bark if he hears suspicious activity at your door or window at 2 a.m., while you're sleeping. On the flip side of that, we have to accept that the dog does not have an "off" switch, so he will sometimes bark at movements or noises that we know are innocuous. Again, the goal is not to stop your dog's barking entirely, especially because then you lose your night guard, but to respond in a way that will calm and reassure him so he chooses to stop barking. The Doorbell Drama section of this chapter (see page 42) addresses management and training strategies to mollify an alarm barker, using the example of barking at the doorbell; however, these strategies can be applied to many other barking scenarios as well. If your dog barks at noises or sights outside your window, the Barking Out the Window section (see page 54) has strategies to help.

There are several other kinds of barking. *Demand barking* or, as I call it, the "bossy bark," can become an irritating habit with some dogs. Bossy barkers are the dogs that look you in the eye and bark at you: "Give me that treat, now!" "Throw that ball for me. Faster, human!" While any dog can demand bark, I see it most frequently with small dogs, those tiny tyrants who simply cannot handle the frustration of being ignored. It's important to address the underlying frustration of demand barking as early as possible. On occasion, dogs whose bossy barks are ignored will then start to jump on you for your attention, then go for a nip of your pants, and so on until someone gets bitten. The Bossy Barker section of this chapter (see page 58) addresses management and training strategies for demand barking.

There is also *excitement barking,* which often happens when you or other beloved humans enter your home. (Depending on the dog, any human could fall into the "beloved" category.) Though we all love being greeted by a wagging, smiling dog, there is no need for rude behaviors like barking, jumping, or biting to be a part of the dog's greeting. The Doorbell Drama section (see page 42) has strategies to address the overly excited doggie greeter.

If your dog is barking consistently when left home alone, the most common causes are boredom or anxiety. (If he only barks occasionally while alone, it may be an alarm bark in reaction to a sudden sound.) *Boredom barking,* repetitive barks in the same mid-range pitch, results when your dog has nothing better to do. Dogs who are cooped up inside a house or apartment all day by themselves may resort to this hobby. *Anxiety barking,* on the other hand, often sounds like a shrill series of barks and sometimes howling, and it can also go on for hours. This kind of barking results when a dog feels uncomfortable, even panicked, being left alone. Anxiety barking is to be taken seriously and usually requires the assistance of a trainer. For all issues related to your dog's being home alone, see Chapter 1.

Resource guarding, shown here, can elicit yet another type of vocalization.

BE PREPARED

Whether you choose the management or training strategies that follow, you'll need to be prepared. You can't always anticipate when your dog will bark—the doorbell just happens to ring, or a neighbor's dog outside your window suddenly begins to yelp, and in an instant your dog is alerting the entire neighborhood. To be ready to train on short notice, keep little tins or bags of treats in all of the places where training might occur. I always keep a tiny bag of treats on a high shelf in the foyer, in a drawer next to my couch, on my desk in the office, and tucked on top of my bed headboard. This way, no matter where I am, I can quickly grab a few treats to train at that very moment. If the doorbell rings, I can't say, "Dogs, can

A durable toy stuffed with food will keep a dog occupied instead of underfoot.

you hold your barking for a minute while I go to the kitchen and get some training treats?" The canine cacophony waits for no one.

To curb barking, as well as many other problematic behaviors, it pays to be prepared with the right training tools. My most valuable training tool is a hollow, durable rubber toy with a large opening that can be filled with peanut butter, plain yogurt, cream cheese, or meat baby food (for human babies, that is). My top choice is peanut butter because the smell is strong and alluring to most dogs. (A word of caution about peanut butter: Check the ingredients to ensure it is free of xylitol, a natural sweetener used in some peanut-butter products as well as in some sugar-free chewing gum, toothpaste, and other sweets. Xylitol is highly toxic to dogs, even in small amounts.) Get a hollow rubber toy that is large enough to be filled with your dog's entire meal in case you want to use his meal as a reward; my dogs weigh about 10 pounds each, and large-sized rubber toys fit their meals perfectly.

Prior to practicing the management and training techniques in this chapter, fill up your toy with either wet or dry food or slather some peanut butter inside and freeze it for a few hours to make the peanut butter harder to lick out. I recommend always having a frozen toy ready in the freezer so you can quickly entertain your dog with a long-lasting food toy when:

- a guest comes over and your dog hasn't learned polite greetings yet;
- you shatter a glass on the floor, and your dog doesn't know Leave It or Place yet;
- there are scary noises, like a thunderstorm, outside, and you want to distract your dog; or
- you receive an important call and want to prevent any barking or bad behavior while you're tied up.

DOORBELL DRAMA

Depending on the dog, the sound of the doorbell can be a source of either excitement or stress—or possibly both. The strategies in this section will help your dog make a new association with the doorbell. Rather than the ringing sound meaning "time to panic," the sound will mean "time for a snack" or "time to sit on my mat." The strategies in this section can address a number of other problems as well, such as jumping on guests who come in, rushing out the door when someone opens it, begging at the table, and demanding attention at inconvenient times.

PROBLEM:
My dog barks and gets overly excited when the doorbell rings.

Management Strategy: Breakfast in Bed

Breakfast in Bed is a simple management technique that you can use when guests are entering your home or any other time you don't want your dog underfoot.

Breakfast in Bed teaches your dog that the trigger (the doorbell) is immediately followed by super-tasty snack in the bedroom or his crate. Being a management strategy, there is technically no training involved, but by practicing the strategy many times, your dog will learn a new association with the doorbell. He has already been classically conditioned to associate the doorbell with excitement or worry about an incoming stranger, which results in barking. Now, you can classically condition him to make a new, calmer association: the sound of the doorbell means he should hurry to the bedroom and wait for his treat-stuffed toy or other time-consuming snack. It's no different from Pavlov's dogs, who learned that a bell predicted food, but in your case, the doorbell predicts food in a certain place that is safely cut off from the excitement of the front door. This management strategy doesn't teach a dog to be well behaved; however, it stops the pattern of going bonkers at the sound of the doorbell, and replaces it with a much more polite and relaxed response of running into the bedroom for a treat. Once the dog is safely behind a closed door, you can let your guest enter and get settled before releasing your dog.

Time-Saving T I P

Make Breakfast in Bed part of your feeding routine so that the doorbell predicts a meal. Prepare the meal first. When you're ready to serve it, ring the doorbell and exclaim, "Breakfast in Bed!"

How to Teach Breakfast in Bed

1. The dog hears the trigger (the doorbell) and you immediately announce, "Breakfast in Bed!"
2. Happily run into the bedroom or to his crate, and give him a pre-stuffed Kong while you secure the door.
3. The dog stays in the room until the distraction is over.
4. In order to be released, you want to ensure the dog is relatively calm. I do this by opening the door a crack and sneaking into the bedroom, and then asking the dog to sit. It might take a few moments, so just stay still until he sits. Then, open the door to release him. In this case, the reward for sitting is being released from the bedroom, so you do not need a treat.

You'll have the best results if you practice the heck out of this before actual guests ring the doorbell. If you don't have a helper to ring the doorbell, record the bell sound on your phone and play that instead. Go through the routine until your dog automatically runs into the bedroom or crate at the sound of the doorbell.

Troubleshooting

Problem: My dog will do it when we practice, but not when real guests come.

Solution: There could be a few reasons for this. First, practice many more times to make sure your dog thoroughly understands the sequence. It can take numerous repetitions before your pooch is ready for real guests, especially if he has a long history of barking at the doorbell. Also, test out different goodies inside the Kong, to see which taste is most irresistible. Some dogs don't care for peanut butter but love cream cheese, and meat baby food is a stinky favorite of most dogs. Finally, when you're expecting visitors, put a note on the door asking them to call you before ringing the doorbell (and then to only ring it once), so you won't be caught off guard and take too long getting the Kong out.

Training Strategy: Place, Level 1 (Duration)

This technique teaches the dog to go to his bed and stay there until released by you. When the dog is in his Place—a designated doggie mat, bed, or crate—he will be concentrating on doing the Place behavior and waiting for your release cue, and as a result, not barking and bouncing around. Place is an example of how we shouldn't just tell a dog, "No, stop barking," but also tell him, "Yes, do this polite behavior instead." By doing the polite behavior of lying on his mat, his excitement level won't escalate nearly as much as if he were jumping at the front door, and as

Teaching Place has lots of practical applications. Here, Batman and Beans are relaxing on their mats rather than getting underfoot while we all enjoy some fresh air and talk about—what else—our dogs!

a result, he won't be inclined to bark his head off while doing Place.

Like Breakfast in Bed, Place is a great way to keep a dog from getting underfoot in any number of situations. Better yet, Place is portable; just bring your dog's mat when you travel, and he'll have a comfy spot to chill even when the surroundings are new and potentially stressful. I always bring my dogs' mats when we travel. For instance, Batman sometimes helps me with lessons at the Brooklyn Dog Training Center, and rather than crate him in a separate room, I simply lay his mat in a corner, where he can nap until I need him. My other dog, Beans, sometimes attends workshops with me, and knowing her mat is a safe place, she is glued to it without any instruction from me. When my dogs and I visit friends who don't like pets on the furniture, having my dogs go to their mats and relax is a way to make everyone happy. The opportunities are endless.

Keep the placement of the mat in mind. If your dog usually barks near the front door, then the mat should be in the vicinity of the action. It's unrealistic to expect your dog to walk to a mat at the other end of your home, and then stay there quietly while all the fun is happening out of sight. I generally keep a mat for each dog in the foyer of my apartment, placed so that they can see what's happening from about ten feet away. If I plan to send them to their mats, say, while I'm cooking, I will simply bring the mats to a corner of the kitchen and the dogs usually settle right in without being asked.

You'll notice that Place is broken up into four levels. This is because it is actually a complicated behavior involving several components your dog must master: he has to sit or lie down for an extended period of time, while you walk away from him, and while some very exciting distractions are happening. For your dog to be successful, break the training up into the Three Ds: duration, distance, and distraction. Only practice one D at a time, so when working on duration (how long your dog is on his mat), it's important to keep the distance between you and the dog short and the distractions low, so he can really focus on increasing the duration.

If your dog doesn't know how to sit or lie down yet, see Chapter 7 and thoroughly teach him at least one of those cues first. (Choose whichever behavior comes more naturally to your dog. There are some dogs who can sit like champs but find lying down on cue awkward. That's fine. Eventually they will get so relaxed that they will lie down on their own.)

How to Teach Place with Duration

1. Pinch a treat between your index finger and thumb, so you are making a pointing gesture. Stand next to mat and lure the dog onto it. Don't say anything yet.

◀ Jacob lures Finn to the mat, using a pointing gesture with a treat wedged between his fingers. Starting with Step 7 of Place, he will remove the treat so that the pointing gesture becomes a cue, not a lure.

◣ Jacob asks Finn to lie down with all four paws on the mat.

▼ Finn gets his reward while he is in the correct position, and then Jacob will release him with "OK."

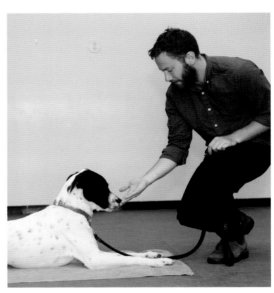

2. Once all of the dog's paws are on the mat, ask for a Sit or Down.
3. When he sits or lies down, mark with "Yes!" and reward. You can let him eat the treat slowly, or feed multiple small treats so he stays on mat for a few moments. Make sure he remains sitting or lying on the mat while he gets the treat.
   - If he pops up to eat the treat, give an NRM (no-reward marker) like "Oops," remove the treat and start over. Revisit Chapter 1 if you're not clear what marking, rewarding, or NRMs are.
4. Release him with "OK" and encourage him to get off the mat.
5. Repeat this until you get four-for-four (meaning, four correct responses in a row, as explained in Chapter 1).

6. This time, add the verbal cue "Place" right before you lure him onto the mat. Repeat steps 1–5.
7. Switch the treat to your other hand, hidden behind your back. Now, as you say "Place," you are pointing to the mat with an empty hand, making it a cue, not a lure. Repeat steps 1–5.
8. Start increasing the amount of time your dog is on the mat. After he gets on the mat, pause for three seconds, give a treat, pause for three seconds, give a treat, pause for three seconds, then mark, reward, and release.

From there, using the rule of four-for-four, gradually build up the duration of Place by adding more seconds between your treats. (Do not add distance or distractions yet.) The goal of this level is for your dog to lie on his mat and get settled while you occasionally give him a treat on his mat. Consider practicing Place with Duration next to a chair or sofa so you can get comfortable and relaxed yourself. Further steps would look something like this:

- Cue him to his Place. Pause five seconds, treat, pause five seconds, treat, pause five seconds, then mark, reward, and release.
- Cue him to his Place. Pause ten seconds, treat, pause ten seconds, treat, pause ten seconds, then mark, reward, and release.
- Continue this pattern until your dog can go at least 30 seconds between treats. Then, start to vary how long the Place lasts; sometimes do a short, easy Place and sometimes do a long one.

I recommend you use the same bed or mat for Place, but move it to many different locations. Dogs do not generalize well, meaning that if you only teach Place in your living room, he won't realize that Place also has the same meaning in other locations. When teaching any behavior in a new location, start from step 1 and work your way up. (Don't worry, it usually progresses faster than the first time you taught it.)

See the Appendix for a sample plan and chart to help you track your progress when training Place, Level 1.

◄ When practicing Place with Distance, make sure your body remains upright, as Jacob's is here.

Training Strategy: Place, Level 2 (Distance)

This level of Place will teach the dog to go to his mat, even when you are not standing next to it. When teaching Place with distance, you will give the "place" cue while standing away from the mat, but remember to return to the mat to mark and reward. Avoid walking away, then releasing your dog or saying "come," followed by a reward; if you do that, what have you rewarded? Not the Place, but rather you've just shown your dog how much fun it is to break away from his Place position and run to you for a treat. By rewarding the dog on his mat, Place becomes inherently rewarding because he only gets his goodies when he's still sitting or lying on his mat. He won't be itching to jump off the mat, and in fact, it might be hard to pry him off it when your training session has finished!

How to Teach Place with Distance

1. If this is your first session of the day, do two or three easy Place Level 1 cues, in which you stand next to the mat, to refresh his memory.
2. This time, take one very small step away from mat. Then, give the Place cue.
   - If your dog hesitates, hold your pointing cue still and look at the mat, not the dog. Give him at least ten seconds to think about what you're asking.
   - Keep your body upright and natural. Avoid reaching unnaturally far; your body should be a step away from the mat, but your hand stretches to reach over it.
3. When your dog sits or lies down on the mat, return to the mat to mark, reward, and release. Make sure he is still in the desired position while eating his treat.
4. Get four-for-four at one small step away.
5. Take another small step away from the mat and repeat the sequence. Get four-for-four.
6. Continue progressing by taking one more small step away, then getting four-for-four.

From there, once your dog has grasped both levels 1 and 2 of Place, you can combine the duration and distance elements. At this point, you don't need to do four-for-four, meaning

you can increase the difficulty slightly after each correct response. However, there is one exception: if your dog struggles at any one step, go back to the previous step and practice it until you get four correct responses in a row. This will ensure you're not moving ahead too quickly. Here is how to incrementally increase the difficulty of both duration and distance combined.

- Take one step away from the mat and cue your dog to do Place. Wait five seconds before you mark, reward, and release. You can shuffle around a little bit while waiting, which looks more natural that simply standing and staring at your dog during that five seconds.
- Take one step away from the mat and cue your dog to do Place. Wait ten seconds before you mark, reward, and release. Break eye contact or shuffle around during the ten seconds.
- Take two steps away from the mat and cue your dog to do Place. Wait five seconds before you mark, reward, and release. Notice how we are now increasing distance but decreasing duration? It's important not to overwhelm your dog by increasing too many criteria at the same time.
- Take two steps away from the mat and cue your dog to do Place. Wait ten seconds before you mark, reward, and release.
- Continue adding both duration and distance, taking care not to substantially increase both aspects in the same rep.

See the Appendix for a sample plan and chart to help you track your progress when training Place, Level 2.

Training Strategy: Place, Level 3 (Distraction)

This level of Place will teach the dog to stay on his mat even when there are distractions present. This requires a lot of impulse control, especially for young or energetic dogs, so work at your dog's pace. It's important to keep the duration and distance low at first; you can always add those elements later. The outline for incorporating all three Ds is laid out after the numbered instructions.

How to Teach Place with Distraction

1. Cue your dog to his Place as before.
2. While he is on his mat, add a small distraction like dropping a small, uninteresting item. (I start with something at "kindergarten level," like an envelope, which won't startle or excite most dogs.) After your dog has remained on his mat during the distraction, mark, reward, and release.
3. Get four-for-four.
4. Gradually work your way up to more distracting items. What constitutes "distracting" depends on the dog, but these are some suggestions:
   - Elementary-school level: lightweight paper goods, like a disposable cup or plate
   - Middle school level: heavier paper goods, like a thin coaster, pamphlet, or placemat
   - Junior-high level: a sock, cloth headband, or hand towel
   - High-school level: a rope toy or old, boring toy
   - College level: a favorite toy, squeaky toy, or ball
   - Master's and PhD level: treats, a rawhide, or pieces of food

Now your pup is getting really good at Place. Vary your practice sessions, systematically increasing one D but keeping the other two about the same as before. At this point, you don't need to do four-for-four, unless your dog struggles at any one step, in which case go back to the previous step and practice it until you get four correct responses in a row. Here are some increasingly challenging variations for combining all three Ds. The part with increasing difficulty is in italics.

DURATION	DISTANCE	DISTRACTION
10 seconds	one step away	Elementary level
10 seconds	*three steps away*	Elementary level
10 seconds	three steps away	*Middle-school level*
20 seconds	three steps away	Middle-school level
20 seconds	*five steps away*	Middle-school level
20 seconds	five steps away	*Junior-high level*

Keep in mind that the above is simply an example, and your dog might need to progress more slowly than this. Work at your dog's level, even if the progress seems slow.

See the Appendix for a sample plan and chart to help you track your progress when training Place, Level 3.

Training Strategy: Place, Level 4 (Doorbell Counterconditioning)

This is the training alternative to Breakfast in Bed. In this case, the doorbell will become the cue for Place to begin. It's easiest to use a recording of your doorbell, so you can start at a low volume and gradually increase it over time. When practicing, if the sound of the doorbell makes your dog react with barking, excitement, or anxiety, then it is too loud. No one can learn when they're in a frenzy, so find a volume that your dog can calmly accept.

How to Teach Place with Doorbell Conditioning

1. Play your recording of the doorbell at a low level. Then, cue Place as before.
2. If your dog is excited, keep the duration and distance short.
3. Get four-for-four.
4. Gradually increase the volume of the doorbell using the rule of four-for-four, until you are able to ring it at full volume and your dog goes to his mat without excitement or anxiety. This could take many sessions to achieve, so be patient and methodical.
5. At this stage, your dog understands that the doorbell means "go to your Place." Now you will cue your dog to his Place, and while he is on that mat, you start walking to the door as if you have a guest. To begin this sequence, use the doorbell to cue Place, and once he is on his mat, take one step towards the front door. Immediately return to your dog to mark and reward, then release. When walking away and then back to your dog, think of

yourself as a boomerang that naturally comes back; it doesn't linger at the end point before returning. Get four-for-four at one step away.

6. Repeat the sequence, but take two steps to the door. Get four-for-four.
7. Continue this until you can reach the door. Get four-for-four at each distance.

Once you get to the door, you will have to practice the most distracting parts of having a guest enter, which involves the door opening and the guest walking in. These steps will all need to be addressed, but remember that if your dog is struggling, you can break it down into even smaller increments.

- Walk to the door and open it a crack, close it, and return to your dog to mark, reward, and release.
- Walk to the door and open it completely, then close it, and return to your dog to mark, reward, and release.
- Walk to the door, open it, say a few words as if you're greeting someone, close the door, and return to your dog to mark, reward, and release.
- Walk to the door, open it, make lots of noises and/or talk loudly, close the door, and return to your dog to mark, reward, and release.
- The final step is to enlist the help of a friend who can act as a calm visitor. You will walk to the door, open it, silently let the guest in, close the door, and return to your dog to mark, reward, and release. After releasing, your dog can greet the calm guest. (If your dog jumps on guests, see Chapter 4.) If your dog jumps off his mat when he realizes an actual guest is there, quickly shut the door (not on your guest's fingers, though!) and start over. It may take a few reps for your dog to realize that any time he jumps up, the door will close and he loses his chance to greet the guest. Get four-for-four.

The front door makes some dogs overly excited.

Training in a Multiple-Dog Household

You can only train a new behavior to one dog at a time. "But Kate," you might say, "you're clearly training three dogs in the photo!" Actually, each of these dogs had already learned Place individually, up through Level 4. This photo captures the first time that Tillie, Batman, and Beans did Place together. Because I have put the dogs in this new multiple-dog scenario, we are doing a full review of Place Level 4, in which I open the door and then shut it.

If you are juggling multiple dogs, follow the same guidelines. Fully train each dog the desired behavior (such as Place) individually. This means that, while training one dog, your other dogs have to be confined in a different room or in their crates. By isolating the dog in training, your progress will move infinitely faster and more smoothly than if you are constantly interrupted by your other dogs while trying to train. Use one of these strategies to keep your other dogs happy while training:

- Use mealtime as training time, so your other dogs are eating from food-dispensing toys for five to ten minutes in another room. Meanwhile, use the meal as rewards for the dog in training.

- Give your other dogs something to occupy their time, like chewies or a new toy, while you train.
- When done training one dog, switch the dogs' places for a few minutes, so your other dogs can have a turn doing training with you, too. (This applies even if your other dogs don't need training. Teach them a fun new trick!)

After all your dogs have become proficient in the desired behavior individually, you can then have the dogs do it together. When asking two or more dogs to simultaneously do Place, Sit, or any other behavior, start at a low level to ensure that they are all successful. Gradually increase the difficulty from there.

Welcome guests into your home with a well-behaved dog and no stress.

- Finally, follow the same sequence, but this time verbally greet the guest as you would in real life. You may need to "split" this into several smaller increments: a very short, quiet greeting at four-four-four, a calm but more natural greeting at four-for-four, and a completely natural, enthusiastic greeting at four-for-four.

A word of caution: It's likely that you'll have visitors coming over before your dog is fully trained in Place. Don't try to do a "PhD-level" Place with a dog who's not ready for it, as you're only setting him up for failure. Instead, rely on Breakfast in Bed to keep him safely in another room until his Place skills are visitor-ready. See the Appendix for a sample plan and chart to help you track your progress when training Place, Level 4, so you'll know when your dog is truly ready for a visitor.

Troubleshooting

Problem: My dog gets up from his mat before I can release him.

Solution: There are two main causes. First, it is possible that you're pushing him beyond his abilities and need to lower your criteria. Make sure that you're methodically implementing four-for-four and working on only one D (distance, duration, or distraction) at a time. In other words, if you're teaching him distance, cueing him to go to his Place from across the room, don't also expect him to stay on his mat for a long duration or while there are distractions in the room. The second cause is for dogs that understand the Place sequence but their rears pop up a moment before you mark and reward. Sometimes dogs get so excited for the reward that they can't sit still at the very end, or perhaps they're looking for a short cut to that treat. In any case, the second his rear comes unglued, use your NRM of "Oops" and stop your approach to reward him. If he quickly plops back down, then you can mark and reward him for kindly correcting his mistake. If he does not correct himself within a second or two, then walk away from him and start over in a few seconds. He's learning that, when he jumps the gun in order to get his treat more quickly, he loses that treat entirely. Bummer! He only gets his reward when he is in the Place position.

Problem: When my guests come in, they get my dog excited and he jumps off his mat.

Solution: If only training humans were as simple as training dogs. Unfortunately, friends and family may lose all self-control when they see those puppy dog eyes staring at them, and their excitement only encourages barking, jumping, and play biting. If you know that guests like this are coming over, it's best to use Breakfast in Bed during their arrival, and only let your dog out once the guests have taken a seat and settled down. This is the strategy I generally take with visitors with high energy or young children whose movements and squeals mimic a giant squeaky toy.

BARKING OUT THE WINDOW

When dogs bark out the window or near your apartment door at people passing by, it can sound vicious. Those dogs often hastily and unfairly get labeled as "aggressive," but in reality, barks in this context can have varied reasons, including alerting the household of a perceived threat, guarding from an "intruder," or feeling frustration at not being able to reach that squirrel hopping around outside. Most barks do not actually lead to bites, and in fact barking is often the dog's attempt to make the threat go away so that he does not have to resort to a bite. (If your dog has bitten guests, however, put down this book and contact a qualified trainer, using the guidelines from Chapter 1.) Regardless of the reason for your dog's barking, the training and management strategies are the same. Each strategy aims not to address the barking itself, but rather to alleviate the underlying stress or excitement that is causing the barking.

My dog barks when people (or dogs or other triggers) pass by the window or front door.

Management Strategy 1: Reduce Triggers

Have you ever tried to kick a bad habit? I remember when I was in my twenties and blissfully unconcerned about my health, and I was drinking cola morning, noon, and night. I was addicted to the stuff. When I finally decided to stop drinking soda, an integral part of my strategy was avoiding triggers. For a while, I only shopped at organic food markets because they didn't sell my beloved drink, I avoided fast food establishments with their alluring free soda refills, and I was "that" friend who brought her own juice or tea to get-togethers. And with every week of a soda-less life, my attitude about soda shifted. Now a decade later, the taste no longer appeals to me. In fact, I can't even drink the stuff without exclaiming like a lightweight, "Whoo, that's bubbly!" Think of your dog's "addiction" to barking out the window in the same way. In addition to the emotional aspect of barking, there is also the habit of the routine: "I hear a noise, I feel stressed, I bark bark bark until it goes away." By reducing the triggers that send your dog into a frenzy, you are taking away his fuel for barking and blocking his ability to feel those stressed emotions.

If people or dogs passing by the window cause your dog stress, close the blinds. If the closed blinds make your home too dark or the dog pokes his nose through them, you can apply a frosted privacy film to all or just the lower part of the window. If your dog is still struggling to see out the window, she is simply not ready to handle having access to that room. Shut doors or use gates to block off any rooms that cause the dog stress.

If it's noise that triggers your dog, add white noise to the room where the problem is. When neighbors in our building were having renovations done, the racket kept my dogs on edge. Once I added white noise in the area with the most banging, the dogs quickly gave up and went back to their usual routine of lounging around. You don't need to buy a white noise machine; a search for "white noise" on YouTube will yield numerous choices for continuous white noise lasting as long as eleven hours. If white noise in the problem area has not reduced your dog's stress after a week, block your dog's access to that area with a fence or gate. Some dogs feel they need to be vigilant in certain areas, especially around the front door, and when you simply don't allow them to spend time in that area, they relax.

Management Strategy 2: Acknowledge the Dog's Concern

Many dogs who bark at someone out the window are doing so to alert you to a potential threat. "Hey, everyone, the mail carrier is out there! Come look!" Ignoring his alert will only lead to more barking because, silly human, you're not acknowledging this very alarming postal worker. Whether or not the threat is real to you doesn't matter; if the threat is real in the dog's mind, then it needs to be addressed.

In my home, the easiest way to extinguish this kind of alarm barking is simply to verbally acknowledge it, which tells my dog that I have it under control. In 2014, my husband and I adopted Beans, a sweet little one-eyed mushball of a mutt who had been saved from deplorable conditions. When she came to live with us in Brooklyn, she was hypersensitive toward every sound and movement in her vicinity. If she heard a car door slam outside, she barked. The neighbor upstairs dropped something, she barked. A leaf fell a half mile away, she barked. Her constant vigilance was frustrating but also heartbreaking. Rather than "shush" her for barking, I acknowledged her concern each time by checking out the noise or movement, calmly saying, "Thanks, Beans, it's OK," and returning to what I was doing. Gradually, the intensity of her barking decreased more and more; after three months or so, a loud thump from upstairs or a barking dog outside got little more than a halfhearted "hmph" from Beans. Now her ears perk up at these sounds, but she no longer needs my reassurance.

How to Acknowledge the Dog's Concern

1. At the first bark towards the window, casually get up and briefly look through the window. If the dog barks at a noise rather than a sight, you can perk up briefly as if listening. Make sure to acknowledge the first bark, before your dog's stress (and noisiness) builds.
2. Turn to your dog and reassuringly say, "Thanks buddy, it's OK," as you return to what you were doing.
3. You can then invite your dog to hang out with you wherever you are. By inviting him to hang out with you, it's changing his focus away from the trigger.

When to Call a Trainer

It's time to contact a trainer if you're feeling frustrated enough to use aversive tools such as a bark-activated e-collar, which automatically administers a shock when the dog barks, or a citronella collar, which automatically sprays a mist in the barking dog's face. I don't even recommend using a spray bottle without speaking to a trainer about what constitutes "training" and what is considered "abuse." As mentioned before, the goal should never be to completely eliminate barking, but rather to find a solution that allows your dog to be a dog, and still lets your neighbors sleep uninterrupted.

It's also time to call a trainer if the dog's barking seems to be escalating in any way. If you see that your dog is getting more and more uncomfortable around triggers, don't wait until the bark becomes a bite. It may be normal—for example, as puppies mature into adolescents, they become more aware of "their" space and may go through a phase in which they regard the world with more caution— but a trainer can help determine how to make your dog more comfortable. If your dog already has a bite history, consult a trainer using the guidelines in Chapter ❶.

Training Strategy: Teach an Alternative Behavior

A commonly used strategy to curb problematic doggie behaviors to to teach a polite, alternative one. As we previously learned, rather than plow grandma down when she comes to visit, your dog could go his Place instead. In the case of barking at outside noises and movement, you probably don't even have to teach your dog anything new. Rather, use an existing behavior your dog knows (such as Sit) and teach him how to do it in a new context. Many of the behaviors in this book can be used to change your dog's focus when he starts to bark: Recall (Chapter 5 and 7), Sit (Chapter 7), Down (Chapter 7), Hand Targeting (Chapter 5), Leave It (Chapter 5), or Place (Chapter 3).

For this strategy to be effective, you'll need to have good timing and some sort of reward nearby. In the early stages of teaching this, I recommend keeping a small sealed container with treats in the places you spend the most time, for instance, near the couch or in a home office. If your dog is toy-motivated, keep a toy there instead, or if your dog goes nuts for your attention, that's a great calorie-free option. The important thing is that the reward is enticing enough to peel your dog's attention away from whatever is setting him off, be it a jogger, a squirrel, or another dog passing by the window. Your dog always has a choice: listen to you, or continue the undesirable behavior of barking. Help him make the "right" choice by paying him in his favorite currency when he chooses to be polite.

How to Teach an Alternative Behavior (Example)
1. Your dog sees a jogger run by the window. Woof, woof, woof!
2. At the first "woof," happily call your dog over to you, and ask him to perform a behavior he knows. For example, "Rocky, come! Good boy! Sit. Good boy!"
3. Reward your dog with a treat, or toss his toy. A short game of fetch or tug will keep him occupied for long enough to forget all about that boring jogger, while reinforcing how cool it is to listen to you.

The purpose of this training strategy is to redirect your dog's focus, which is easiest to do if you catch him after the first bark, so his emotions don't get out of hand. Don't wait for ten seconds of barking, because a dog that's having a full-on meltdown is not a dog you can train. With consistency, when your dog hears the trigger, he'll skip the barking and come right over to you for his reward. What a great choice he made! Give that dog a bone.

Troubleshooting
Problem: My dog won't listen to me when I call him away from the window.

Solution: This generally has one of two causes.
1. Your rewards don't cut it. If you're asking your dog to perform a behavior that's really hard for him (and concentrating on you when there is a jogger whizzing by is hard), we need to pay him accordingly. If you are a stingy

boss, your employees will find a better job; likewise, if you give stingy rewards, your dog will choose the jogger over you.

2. The distraction of the jogger is too intense for your dog to ignore. This simply means you need to practice this routine with less intense triggers at first. While your dog is mildly distracted by a noise or activity, call him over and ask him to sit, and give him his reward. Repeat this many times until it becomes an awesome game. Once the game becomes second nature, he'll have a much easier time following the same steps during a more intense distraction. In the meantime, if an intense distraction pops up, help him out by going to him and gently leading him back to the spot where he sits for his reward.

BOSSY BARKER

Similar to humans, dog personalities run the gamut. On one given day I might work with a nervous Dachshund that reminds me of Woody Allen, a turbo-charged Pit Bull reminiscent of Robin Williams, and a sassy Pomeranian who must have taken lessons in confidence from Madonna herself. There are some dogs out there who are, to put it plainly, bossy. While many dogs may never bark to get your attention, there are others who quickly learn the power of their voices. Why do they bark at you when they want that treat in your hand or the ball that rolled under the couch? Because it works! Many of us will give the dog what he is barking for, either to stop the barking before the neighbors get annoyed, or just because we want to please our dogs.

Based on their inherent cuteness, it's easy to get caught in the trap of seeing your dog as a baby throughout his whole life. And while he does depend on you for all his needs and gives

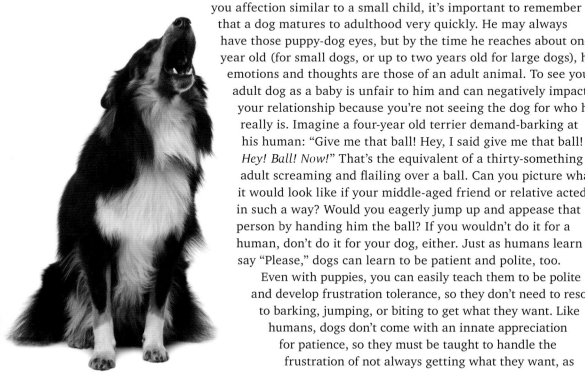

you affection similar to a small child, it's important to remember that a dog matures to adulthood very quickly. He may always have those puppy-dog eyes, but by the time he reaches about one year old (for small dogs, or up to two years old for large dogs), his emotions and thoughts are those of an adult animal. To see your adult dog as a baby is unfair to him and can negatively impact your relationship because you're not seeing the dog for who he really is. Imagine a four-year old terrier demand-barking at his human: "Give me that ball! Hey, I said give me that ball! *Hey! Ball! Now!*" That's the equivalent of a thirty-something adult screaming and flailing over a ball. Can you picture what it would look like if your middle-aged friend or relative acted in such a way? Would you eagerly jump up and appease that person by handing him the ball? If you wouldn't do it for a human, don't do it for your dog, either. Just as humans learn to say "Please," dogs can learn to be patient and polite, too.

Even with puppies, you can easily teach them to be polite and develop frustration tolerance, so they don't need to resort to barking, jumping, or biting to get what they want. Like humans, dogs don't come with an innate appreciation for patience, so they must be taught to handle the frustration of not always getting what they want, as well as learn to ask for what they want politely. The strategy for puppies and adults is the same, and if you implement these concepts from day one, you will likely prevent demand barking altogether. In essence, the following strategies teach that polite dogs get what they want, while rude dogs get zilch, nada, nothing. The management and training strategies in this section go hand in hand; you will likely need to employ both to make it clear to your dog that certain calm behaviors will work for him and other disruptive behaviors won't.

When working to extinguish demand barking, be aware of a tricky thing called an extinction burst, in which the barking actually gets worse before it dies out. Imagine a toddler who has a history of throwing tantrums in a toy store and who is rewarded for his screaming by getting a toy each time. When, one day, his parents finally stop acquiescing to his demands, the tantrum may actually escalate—more screaming and thrashing than ever before—because his old strategy isn't working anymore. This is the grand finale of the tantrum, after which the child is usually much more amenable. If you find that your dog's barking gets more intense when you finally start to ignore him, it is likely an extinction burst. Following this, the dog will react much more quietly because he has realized that this doggie tantrum no longer works. (If your dog's frustrated behavior tips into anything dangerous, like biting, contact a trainer using the guidelines in Chapter 1.)

PROBLEM:
My dog looks at me and barks when he wants something: food, a toy, to be let outside, and so on.

Management Strategy 1: Ignore All Rude, Demanding Behavior
Combined with the training strategies below, this will teach your pup that demand barking doesn't work. He is barking because wants your attention, and starting today, when he demand barks, he loses your attention. He gets the opposite of what he wants. He gets ignored. This means you will not say anything to him, not even "No!" or "Shhh," because for a demand barker, even negative attention will add fuel to his fire. When dogs teach each other to be polite, they use their body language, not their words, so your dog will understand by your actions that his barking has an undesired consequence.

How to Ignore, Level 1
1. The moment he begins barking at you to demand something, turn your head away and break eye contact. Act as if his demand barking is your "off" switch, automatically turning off your attention while he is barking. Don't say anything.
2. When he stops barking, you can reward him with the thing he wants. He is learning that only quiet dogs get what they want. I recommend adding the Bossy Barker training strategies to this step, which will replace barking with a polite behavior your dog can do when he wants something.
3. Repeat this sequence every single time your dog demand barks. If you occasionally give in to his demand barking, it can actually make the barking more persistent by building up his stamina. (He thinks to himself, "Last time she caved in after I barked for a long time, so I'm going to bark even longer until she caves this time.")

Kenzi: Bossy Barker Extraordinaire

Kenzi is a Miniature Schnauzer whose sweet face belies her ability to bark so loudly that your ears will ring. Her owners, Eric and Abi, love Kenzi dearly, but they were visibly frustrated and exhausted when I arrived at their house for the first private lesson. And they had good reason—Kenzi had been waking them up every morning at 4 a.m., whining, jumping on and off the bed, and pacing to demand her breakfast.

Problem: Kenzi's demands for food were affecting the couple's sleep, morning routine, and, not surprisingly, their patience. Her cries started earlier and earlier, and Abi would get up to feed Kenzi between 4 and 5 a.m. so that they could all go back to sleep. The feeding ritual itself was no better; while Abi prepared the food, Kenzi wailed, barked, and bounced.

Solution: Having ruled out medical or other causes for her behavior, we tackled Kenzi's bossy barking from several angles.

- **Early-morning solutions:** Kenzi lost her bed privileges, at least for the time being. We thoroughly conditioned her to love her dog bed (by giving her all kinds of goodies while on that bed), which became her new sleeping spot. Additionally, the couple managed the space by padding the floor with area rugs to reduce the click-click-click sound of Kenzi's nails, should she start pacing. Finally, Eric and Abi practiced Level 2 of ignoring her demand whining. If Kenzi walked over to the bed and cried for food, they turned away from her and refused to acknowledge her demands.

- **Feeding-routine solutions:** First, we changed the order of Kenzi's morning activities. No one was to get out of bed before Abi's alarm went off at 6 a.m. (which is early enough!). Abi took care of her own needs first, brushing her teeth and getting dressed. After that, she took Kenzi out for a walk. Then, they practiced Place with Duration in the kitchen while Abi prepared Kenzi's breakfast. This broke the pattern of "I cry and pace, and then you feed me," replacing it with a routine in which food came only after a walk and as a result of the polite behavior of Place.

Kenzi picked up this new routine almost immediately, and, within a few days, everyone had acclimated to the new rules and was getting more sleep. Furthermore, while Kenzi was in her place, awaiting breakfast, she was so focused on staying put that her barking had reduced dramatically. If Eric and Abi keep up their good work and never give in to her predawn demands, I'm hopeful that Kenzi will be invited back into the bed in the future.

Depending on the dog, you might be able to stop here. Once your dog realizes that barking triggers your "off" switch and you will not respond, his barking will extinguish over time. However, some dogs have a long history of barking and could go on for hours before they realize it's not working. In an urban situation surrounded by neighbors, you may not have the ability to stand there while your dog barks his head off indefinitely. In this case, levels two and/or three might be necessary.

How to Ignore, Level 2

This level may be necessary for dogs who also get physical when they demand your attention, for example, a large dog who jumps up.

1. The moment your dog starts to bark, turn away from him so your back is facing him. If you are sitting in a chair, stand up and turn away. Stay still and silent, like a statue, and don't move away from the dog. This is a higher-level snub than in level one, and it protects you from getting your face or chest scratched if he jumps.
2. When he stops barking, you can reward him with the thing he wants. He is learning that only quiet dogs get what they want. I recommend adding the Bossy Barker training strategies to this step, which will replace barking with a polite behavior your dog can do when he wants something.
3. Repeat this sequence every single time your dog demand barks.

How to Ignore, Level 3

This is the highest level of ignoring, which I reserve for the most determined demand barkers.

1. The moment your dog starts to bark, walk away into another room and shut the door behind you. Count to ten. Then, as long as your dog is not barking anymore, return to what you were doing. (If your dog keeps up barking, stay in the other room until he stops.) When you return to what you were doing, act as if nothing had happened; just go back to your emailing or laundry-folding. Stay silent the entire time.
2. When you're ready to give him what he wants, first ask him to do a polite behavior as outlined in the following training strategies. A polite behavior is the only way to get what he wants.
3. Repeat this sequence every single time your dog barks.

Management Strategy 2: That's All

Teaching your dog a cue that means "that's all; no more attention for you" is a simple technique that can make a significant improvement in your dog's behavior. Part of the reason dogs beg, demand, and jump on you for attention (or for food, or for a toy) is because we give them certain goodies but don't tell them when the goodies have stopped coming their way. As a result, the dog keeps pushing for more. Dogs, by nature, are scavengers, so they're programmed to stare at us while we eat or wait for us to drop a piece of food as we put away the leftovers. I don't have a problem with being watched while I cook or eat; honestly, for a cooped-up city dog, watching you prepare food might be the highlight of his day. And, brace yourself—I don't even have a problem with giving your dog little bits of your food. That being said, there have to be some rules to prevent bossy barking, jumping, or counter-surfing when your back is turned.

When I am cooking, I have my dogs doing Place on mats in a corner of the kitchen, where they can watch the action but are not underfoot. On my "healthy" days, I dutifully drag out my kale and other veggies from the fridge, at which point Beans's face lights up because she loves kale more than anything else in this world. (We joke that she is "so Brooklyn" now.) As I'm making my salad, I always tear off a piece of kale and give it to each dog while they are on their mats, though Batman usually snubs his piece. A few moments later, with both dogs still doing Place, I might toss each one a slice of carrot. When I'm finished sharing with them, I tell them "That's all" and go back to my meal prep. The dogs know that this means they won't be getting any more food, so they settle down on their mats. Had I not said "That's all," they might continue to be on edge, waiting for the possibility of another piece. This can lead to excitement or frustration, which in turns leads to their breaking their Place and potentially barking at me or jumping up to get more food.

How to Teach That's All

1. Give your dog a treat (he does not have to "do" anything for it). Pause for a few seconds and then give him a second treat.
2. Once he's eaten the second treat, say "That's all" and use a hand gesture unique to this cue. My hand gesture is my two hands crossing horizontally like a baseball umpire doing the "safe" gesture. Some people prefer to shrug or to show their empty hands.
3. As soon as you make your unique gesture, turn or walk away from the dog. If he barks or jumps up, use Management Strategy 1 (ignoring). He will learn that once you say "That's all," he has zero chance of getting any more of that treat, so there is no need for him to cry or beg.

You can then apply That's All to a wide variety of situations.

- Pet your dog for a minute. Say "That's all" and do your gesture, and then stop all petting. Ignore your dog's pushy attempts to make you pet him again.
- Play a game of fetch or tug with your dog. When you get tired of the game, say "That's all" and show him your gesture, and then walk away. Ignore your dog if he tries to engage you in the game again.
- When training, some dogs get so focused on the rewards that training actually becomes difficult. At that point, it's a good time for a break, so tell your dog "That's all" and show him your gesture, and then stop training for a few minutes. Let your dog do something else, like play a game or have a drink of water, to relax a bit.

When practicing That's All, keep in mind that once you say it, you have to follow through. It will only confuse your dog if you tell him "That's all" and then change your mind and give him another cookie.

Training Strategy 1: Check Me Out

Revisit the Check Me Out game from Chapter 2. Use this technique any time your dog wants anything from you, such as food, toys, getting his leash clipped, or opening the door. The purpose of Check Me Out is to teach your dog that eye contact, not jumping or barking or

◄ Mealtime is a great way to teach your dog Sit for It. Here, Malik Jr. will only get his meal if he sits politely while Rachel puts his bowl down.

◣ Malik Jr. is looking into the bowl, but his rear end is still firmly on the ground. Good boy! (If he had stood up, Rachel would have removed the bowl and started over.)

▼ Once Rachel has fully stood up, she says "OK" to give Malik Jr. permission to eat his meal.

nipping, gets him what he wants every time. When practicing the ignoring management strategies for demand barking, you can insert Check Me Out into Step 2. Once the dog has stopped barking, he has to look at you as if to say "Please," and only then will you give him what he wants.

Training Strategy 2: Sit for It

Similar to Check Me Out, having your dog sit for whatever he wants is a simple way to teach him to be polite in all situations. Lulu wants you to throw a ball? Sure, but she's got to sit for it first. You will ignore all barking and yapping, only throwing the ball once she sits. Time for

Miles's dinner? Great! He'll need to sit while you prepare it and put it on the floor. If he barks or jumps up, stop preparing it and ignore him until he is sitting again. Sit for It complements the ignoring strategy well because we're not just telling the dog not to bark; we're also telling him what to do instead. Consequently, we replace a disruptive behavior with a polite one. Once your dog learns that polite sitting gets him what he wants, he will be sitting for everything, and you won't even have to ask. Now that's a good dog!

How to Teach Sit for It

1. Hold out a treat. You can maintain gentle eye contact with your dog, but don't say anything. Wait for him to sit, ignoring any rude behavior, such a jumping or barking.
2. The moment he sits, mark and reward with that treat. Your dog has just learned that his rude actions got him nothing, and his polite sitting got him exactly what he wanted.

You'll notice that in the instructions, I did not use the verbal cue "Sit." By not telling the dog exactly what to do, it pushes him to think for himself. *Hmm, what do I have to do to get that treat? Barking didn't work. Jumping didn't work. Maybe I'll sit and see if that works.*

Whenever possible, I encourage the dog to problem-solve his way through an issue rather than simply obeying my cue, which doesn't require as much thinking on his part. In my experience, a dog who is allowed to find a solution himself (for instance, discovering that sitting or eye contact gets rewards) can apply that information more quickly and to more contexts than a dog who is always told what to do. That being said, if your dog is too excited or distracted to figure out by himself that sitting "works," then, by all means, cue him to sit.

From there, repeat this exercise with everything your dog wants. Does he like to play tug? If so, hold out the toy to initiate the game and wait for him to sit. The moment he sits, the game can start. Does he like to lounge with you on the couch? That's fine, but only if he sits and waits for your invitation. If he jumps on the couch without being asked, gently remove him, put him back on the floor, and wait for him to ask politely before inviting him up. (You can only enforce this rule while you're sitting on the couch.) In a short time, most dogs start sitting for everything they want. It becomes a default behavior and replaces demand barking, jumping, and nipping.

Troubleshooting

Problem: My dog will sit (or give eye contact if doing Check Me Out), but he simultaneously barks at me.

Solution: Sitting is only polite if it's done quietly, so withhold marking and rewarding until your dog has stopped barking. This might take some patience, but the best thing to do is simply stand there, toy or treat in hand, and wait for your dog to realize that his barking isn't working. Resist the urge to repeat "Sit, sit, sit"—instead, let your dog figure it out for himself. If your dog is really carrying on, you can start by marking and rewarding even a brief intermission between barks. As time goes on, tighten the criteria to require a one-second pause between barks, then a two-second pause, and so on.

DOGS OF Ⓑ Ⓚ Ⓛ Ⓝ

Meet Malik Jr.

Malik Jr., Facebook star and melter of hearts worldwide, was found tied to a pole in Brooklyn in December 2015. After ending up at Animal Care Center (the city shelter), Malik Jr. was taken in by Red Hook Dog Rescue and fostered by Rachel, a volunteer who instantly fell for this gentle boy. Rachel recalls, "Fostering lasted all of twenty-four hours; that's how long it took me to realize he wouldn't be going anywhere else."

Malik Jr., whose unique name came from his previous owner's microchip, fit right in with his new canine brother and sister, also rescues. He is an easygoing Bulldog who always stops to smell the roses—and, to him, everything seems to be a rose. Rachel remembers that "initially, Malik Jr. would not walk on a leash. He would also just refuse to move when I called him or when he didn't want to leave [somewhere] fun, like the dog park or a park bench." Hand Targeting (Chapter ⑤) has worked wonders to get Malik Jr. "unstuck" from his resting spots. Rachel uses a series of hand targets to get him up and moving, and then she rewards him with a high-value treat for his hard work (bananas are his favorite!). His canine sister, who is more active, helps encourage Malik Jr. to get his motor running, too.

4

K

KNOCKING
PEOPLE OVER

K Keep Your Paws to Yourself

Even with small dogs, jumping up can be a problematic behavior.

You've probably noticed that some dogs don't have much regard for personal space. But muddy paws have no place on the neighbor's dry-clean-only blazer, and large dogs who jump can present a danger to kids or the elderly. So I have a zero-tolerance policy related to jumping, and that includes *all* friends and family members, even the ones who like when dogs jump on them. Allowing Leroy to jump on some but not all people is confusing and unfair to him; how can you expect him to follow the rule when the rule changes? In situations like this, Grandma will inevitably be knocked over, and Leroy will wonder what kind of strange world he is living in, where he is rewarded with attention when he jumps on some people but punished for jumping on others.

Can you still pet your dog and show your affection? Of course! Isn't that why you got a dog in the first place? This chapter will give you several management and training strategies to teach your dog that he gets all the attention he wants when he's being polite, with four paws firmly on the ground. Polite greetings are a win-win for both dog and human. The strategies for the first problem in this chapter pertain to outdoor scenarios, while the second problem focuses on indoor jumping.

Note that these strategies are intended for dogs who jump because they are overly enthusiastic greeters. These strategies should not be used on dogs who are lunging at or jumping on people in an unfriendly way (as if to say "Back off!"), nor should these strategies be used on shy dogs who jump on their handlers because they are afraid of something in their surroundings.

PROBLEM:
When I'm walking my dog, he jumps on every person who walks by.

Management Strategy 1: Practice Your "New Yorker Walk"
The New Yorker walk is the gait of a person on a mission. It sends a clear message to both your dog and to other people on the street that you aren't interested in stopping for small talk. When you see a potential distraction up ahead, such as a stranger or another dog, start your New Yorker walk ahead of time to prevent an interaction your dog isn't calm enough to handle.

The New Yorker walk has four components:

- Body-block the dog. This means you'll put yourself between the dog and any distraction. For many dogs, using your body as a barrier sends the message that they won't physically be able to jump on the oncoming person, so they don't even try. This strategy works for other distractions, as well. You can body-block between your dog and another dog, a kid on a skateboard, or a squirrel hopping along your route.
- Have a short enough leash that the dog can't swerve and drag you. I recommend tying a knot in your leash about midway, or closer to the clip for taller dogs. This allows you to immediately get into New Yorker mode by grabbing the knot, so you have the perfect leash length without any fumbling. (You can also buy a leash with an additional handle built in near the clip.)

> # A Word about Walks
>
> I'm going to sound like a downer here, but until your jumpy dog is well trained, I strongly encourage you not to let him even have the chance to greet people passing by. If your dog knows he can drag you from person to person, then that becomes the focus of his walks. You become invisible to your dog because you're not nearly as interesting as all these new friends he's dying to meet. It's also not fair to allow your dog to greet people sometimes, but not all the time. How is he supposed to know which ones are fair game? Don't confuse your yet-to-be-trained dog—just keep on walking, for everyone's sake. Attention from passersby is a privilege, not a right, and once he's learned not to jump, he can have all the petting he wants. (Note: If your dog's Achilles heel is controlling himself around other dogs rather than humans, Chapter ⑤ has got your covered.)

◀ Joe and Susu show us the appropriate leash length for the New Yorker Walk. It has a little slack but does not give Susu the freedom to swerve around her handler.

▼ Jacob steps on the leash so that Finn can comfortably stand but not jump up to greet the "friendly stranger." Be ready to implement this management technique before your dog starts to jump.

- Avoid eye contact with the approaching person. This is a time-tested New York solution to preventing all kinds of awkward confrontations. If a full snub is too coldhearted for you, cast your eyes toward your dog when passing someone and gently tell your pup how well he's behaving. This gives people the impression that you're training (which you are!), and passersby are unlikely to interfere.
- Set a fast pace and don't slow down. Don't stroll like a tourist; be on a mission!

Management Strategy 2: Step on the Leash

This one is simple. Provided that your leash is long enough (and a regular 6-foot lead will suffice), you will step on the middle portion of the leash so your dog physically can't jump up. The intention is not to hurt the dog, so refer to the equipment section of Chapter 5 to make sure your dog is wearing a safe harness or collar for this activity. The purpose is simply to stop the undesirable behavior—to break the habit of jumping. Since jumping on people is inherently fun for dogs, the behavior becomes more firmly ingrained in the dog's repertoire with every jump. What starts as an experiment quickly becomes habitual and, thus, harder to break. And, as you've probably learned, strangers are generally terrible at following your instructions not to pet your jumping dog. These well-meaning people further reinforce the dog's jumping by rewarding him with attention when he jumps on them. Consequently, the responsibility all falls to you, the handler, to keep your pup from jumping.

How to Step on the Leash

1. When you cannot avoid a greeting, pull over and collect yourself before the stranger approaches. Don't wait for your dog to start going bonkers.
2. Step on a midway point of your leash so that your dog can comfortably stand but not jump up.
3. Once you've prevented your dog from jumping, the stranger can reach down to pet him.

This technique is only a temporary fix for dogs in the early stages of learning not to jump, and it can be used in conjunction with the training strategies that follow. Once your dog has developed more self-control through training, you will no longer need to step on the leash.

Training Strategy 1: Four on the Floor

This training strategy is best if you have family members or friends who can help you practice. You're going to teach your dog that all the attention from humans comes when he has four paws firmly on the floor. The moment his front paws start flailing, the attention stops and the person walks away. Bummer! The best part about this strategy is that the person's attention is the reward, so it's calorie-free training with no need for treats.

How to Teach Four on the Floor

This exercise requires two people, one holding the dog on leash and one acting as a "friendly stranger" who approaches the dog. The dog and his handler remain still, while the friendly stranger will move toward the dog. The following instructions are for the friendly stranger; the handler does not need to do anything.

1. Walk toward the dog calmly. If the dog is very excitable, don't make eye contact.
2. If the dog rears up at any point, turn and walk away. His actions just lost him the chance to get your attention.
3. If the dog has four paws on the floor, reward him with gentle petting. If he jumps up during the petting, game over! Walk away.

Once your dog can handle a calm approach for four repetitions in a row, you can gradually intensify your excitement level. These are some possible steps:

- Make eye contact and smile at the dog as you approach. Get four-for-four.
- If that goes well, talk to him a little as you get closer. Get four-for-four.
- Talk gently to him and use low, inviting body language with slightly outstretched arms. Get four-for-four.
- Continue making your approaches more enthusiastic by adding more sound or expressive body language.

Each person who practices should follow the same routine, starting with a calm approach. Dogs don't generalize well, so you'll need to practice this with several different people until your dog realizes, *Ohhh, you mean this rule applies to all humans!* See the Appendix for a sample plan and chart to help you track your progress when training Four on the Floor.

Troubleshooting

Problem: My dog can't sit still even when I calmly approach.

Solution: Lower your criteria. With extra-bouncy dogs, sometimes you have to start by walking toward him in an indirect, curving path, similar to how polite dogs greet each other. Swing a wide loop toward the dog so you actually make contact with him by approaching his shoulder rather than his head. Avoid eye contact and try to keep your arms still or folded. Essentially, try to be as boring as possible.

Training Strategy 2: Sit for Greeting

If Four on the Floor is a little too complicated for your friends and family, don't despair. This next strategy only requires one person—you—to be on the ball. In this scenario, the dog must remain sitting while a friendly stranger approaches. Because, initially, this will be difficult for your dog to do, use delicious treats to reward him for his hard work.

Sitting to greet is an example of what trainers call "teaching an incompatible behavior." If your dog is sitting when a stranger approaches, by default he isn't jumping or lunging (he can't sit and jump at the same time). You have successfully stopped the rude behavior without using force, and you've reinforced how rewarding it is to be polite instead. With consistency, you will have a dog that sees a stranger and automatically sits in anticipation of a greeting.

The goal of this exercise is to condition your dog to look to you when a person approaches. Rather than thinking, *Woohoo! Someone to jump on!*, we want him to think, *Woohoo! Someone's coming! Time to look at my human and sit for goodies!* To make the connection that strangers equal goodies, you will start this activity at the moment your dog sees the stranger approaching. Don't wait for your dog to start jumping and pulling toward the person; you've already lost his attention at that point. Rather, if you ask for the polite behavior before your dog starts to lose control, you are preventing the problem from even starting and teaching a calmer, more polite greeting routine.

How to Teach Sit for Greeting

Though the instructions below use the word *stranger* to describe an approaching person, this strategy works just as well with people your dog already knows.

1. The moment your dog notices a stranger approaching on the sidewalk, tell him to sit. If he is already excited, you might need to lure him into the Sit by putting the treat in front of his nose. That's fine in the beginning.

While the "stranger" pets Susu, Joe gives her several pieces of cheese. Susu is much more interested in the cheese than the stranger; with a little practice, she'll learn that sitting for strangers is more rewarding than jumping on them.

2. As the stranger approaches, continue treating as frequently as needed. At first, it will probably look like a rapid-fire treat-treat-treat with few or no pauses in between.

3. When the stranger reaches you, it's up to you if she can pet your pooch. Don't feel obligated to let it happen. Remember that your responsibility is to your dog, not to a passerby who you will never see again. A quick, "Sorry, we're training" and then breaking eye contact with the person is perfectly acceptable.

4. If you agree to the petting, continue the rapid-fire treating through the encounter. Don't worry if your dog gets up and stands at this point, as long as all four paws are on the ground.

5. The moment the interaction is over, stop treating and briskly walk away on a short leash. Don't give your dog the chance to try to follow, nip at, or jump on the person as she walks away.

Once your dog starts to figure out that an approaching stranger signals treats, he will see a stranger coming and, rather than fixate on this new friend, will look at you. This means he's catching on. Good dog! While he's looking at you, ask him for a Sit and start rewarding—but how much should you reward once he starts to figure out the "game"? Let's say your dog can sit through the encounter with the strangers (or at least sit while the person approaches and stand up for the actual petting, if you allow it). You can now start to reduce how frequently you have to treat your pooch to keep his rear on the ground and his focus on you. As time goes on, your rapid-fire treating will become treat-pause-treat-pause-treat. Once your dog can ace short pauses between treats, reduce it to treat-pause-pause-treat-pause-pause-treat. With time and repetition, the pauses get longer and longer as the dog gains more self-control.

Work at your dog's pace as you increase the pauses between treats; for some dogs, it might take only a few sessions, or, for a dog or puppy like Pogo (described in the Introduction), it

could take several weeks. When it comes to reducing your treats, don't rush it. If your dog starts breaking his Sit, it means you have reduced the frequency of treats too quickly, and he has become confused. See the Appendix for a sample plan and chart to help you track your progress when training Sit for Greeting.

Troubleshooting
Problem: My dog can't sit still. He keeps popping up.

Solution: There are three possible reasons and solutions.

- Your rate of reinforcement (how frequently you treat) needs to be more rapid-fire. If your dog loses focus when you pause between treats, it means your pauses are too long. Just as children learn the alphabet before they can build longer words or sentences, many dogs need to begin with a foundation of continuous treats to keep them focused before they can handle longer pauses between treats.
- You need higher-level treats. Make sure you're treating with something delicious, like pieces of chicken, hot dogs, or string cheese, as frequently as it takes to keep your dog focused on you. Kibble might work when training indoors or in low-distraction environments, but

Doing Nothing Is Really Something!

While making online training videos to demonstrate some of the *BKLN Manners*™ strategies, my husband/videographer made an interesting comment. After filming a minute or two of me having Beans sit when she spotted a passerby, he said, "So when are you and the dog going to do anything?" This observation gave me an "Aha!" moment because, when properly training a dog to be well behaved, it indeed looks as if you and the dog are doing nothing at all.

With many of the strategies in this book, the goal is to help your dog stop doing any number of undesirable actions, like barking or jumping. The solution, of course, is a calm behavior, like sitting, giving you eye contact, or simply eating a treat in the presence of a trigger (which you will see in the Counterconditioning section of Chapter ⑤). These behaviors don't look terribly impressive to the untrained eye, but, in reality, when a dog is learning to control his impulses and perform a polite behavior, he is working very hard. For some dogs, in fact, doing a short Sit-Stay on the sidewalk is infinitely harder than a trick like standing up on his hind legs and spinning in a circle.

So, if someone ever raises an eyebrow at your impulse-control training and claims that your dog isn't doing anything but sitting, it's fine to respond, "Thank you for the compliment!"

if your dog isn't interested in his kibble when you're training around distractions, it's a clear signal that he needs better payment for the effort he's putting in.

- Your dog can't yet handle sitting in this level of distraction. At this point, start practicing Sit outdoors when there are no distractions so he learns how much fun it is to sit on cue. Repeat it so often that sitting becomes a part of your dog's repertoire. Meanwhile, use the management strategies in this chapter when you're passing people on the street so your dog isn't given the opportunity to jump on passersby. Once your dog responds consistently to the Sit cue on your walks, you can ask him to sit in the presence of distractions, such as approaching strangers.

Problem: My dog will sit for some people but not others.

Solution: Be selective. Not all strangers are suitable to greet your dog, particularly excited kids and those overly enthusiastic "it's-OK-I-love-all-dogs" adults. Sometimes, looking out for your dog's best interests means snubbing a human (politely, of course). But, let's face it—those humans don't think twice about undoing all your hard work by encouraging your dog to jump, so don't feel badly if you ask them to keep on walking.

Training Strategy 3: Let's Shake on It

Perhaps your pup is the life of the party, making human friends wherever he goes. It's understandable that you don't want to take away all of his social interaction. One way to harness your dog's exuberance is to teach him a cool interactive trick that is incompatible with jumping. My favorite, and often the easiest to train, is Shake (or Give Paw). The beauty of Shake is that it allows both parties, the dog and the human, to interact politely with each other. If your dog can shake for a new friend, he can't simultaneously be jumping, and the person on the receiving end of the shake will have no need to encourage your dog to jump up. Win-win! Many dogs love this behavior and offer it to everyone without even being cued.

How to Teach Shake

There are many ways to teach this behavior, and here I explain two different ways. I recommend trying the former method first because it requires your dog to figure out Shake for himself.

1. Ask your dog to sit.
2. Hide a treat in one hand. Extend that hand with your palm up, but in a loose fist to protect the treat, to the sitting dog.
3. Ignore any mouthing at your hand. When the dog paws at your hand, mark and reward.
4. Get four-for-four.
5. Add the cue "Shake" right before you present your fist. Get four-for-four.
6. Remove the treat from your fist and put it in your other hand, which is hidden behind your back. Say "Shake" and extend your empty fist. When he shakes, reward from your other hand. Get four-for-four.
7. Gradually open your cue hand. Take it slowly, opening your palm an inch or so more each

◄ Ilyssa presents a treat in her fist, palm up. At first, Susu just wants the treat, so she licks and paws at the fist. The moment Susu's paw touches Ilyssa's hand, it magically opens, and Susu gets the treat. (Hold your fist where your dog can easily paw at it.)

◄ Susu is getting the idea. At Step 6, Ilyssa's fist is empty; she will reward Susu with a treat hidden in her pocket.

◄ At Step 7, Ilyssa has started opening her hand a little more with each rep.

time you give the Shake cue. If you go immediately from a fist to a flat palm, your dog probably won't understand this dramatically different cue. If your dog gets stuck, go back to the previous step (a tighter fist) and get four-for-four.

The following method works for dogs whose paws seem glued to the ground. It's less desirable than the foregoing method because you're doing the work for the dog, which doesn't help build his independent-thinking skills.

1. Ask your dog to sit.
2. Extend one hand, palm up, in the Shake gesture. Meanwhile, with your other hand, tap the back of one of the dog's lower front legs.
3. When he feels the pressure of your tap and lifts the leg up, let his paw briefly touch or rest in your outstretched palm. Mark and reward. Get four-for-four.
4. Add the cue "Shake" before this sequence, so it is "Shake," present your open palm, lightly tap the back of the leg, and mark and reward when the dog's paw touches your palm. Get four-for-four.
5. With each rep, tap the back of your dog's leg more lightly each time until you don't need to tap at all.

Troubleshooting

Problem: My dog is too excited to shake strangers' hands.

Solution: Rome wasn't built in a day, so be patient. Start practicing this in low-distraction areas, with just you and the dog. Practice with friends and family indoors before testing it outdoors. When you do transfer Shake to outdoor scenarios, your dog might be too distracted to focus, so start from the beginning and work your way back up. Outside, cue your dog to shake with you and with others he already knows so that his excitement level is manageable. With time and practice, your dog will generalize the behavior, which means he'll be able to do it in all different situations as well as with new people.

Remember, the more you reward a behavior, the more often a dog will do it. If Shake gets the dog a lot of cookies and attention, it can become his default behavior around new people. And then you become the coolest dog owner on the block.

PROBLEM:
My dog jumps on my guests, especially as they're coming into my home.

Management Strategy: Breakfast in Bed
Remember this strategy from Chapter 3? Breakfast in Bed is an effective strategy for a dog who jumps on your guests as they enter or move about your home. By sending the dog to his crate or another room and entertaining him with a treat-dispensing toy, you've prevented the jumping and saved your guests from getting slobbered on.

Breakfast in Bed is often the first line of defense for overly enthusiastic greeters. Since the training methods that follow require some time to build up a dog's impulse control, you can use Breakfast in Bed starting today. This management strategy does not "cure" the dog of his jumping because it doesn't actually teach him to do anything polite. However, by removing your dog from the excitement of the front door, you are preventing the problem from escalating because he is not able to make a habit out of jumping on people. This, in turn, will make your training easier. See the instructions for Breakfast in Bed in Chapter 3.

Training Strategy 1: Sit for Greeting
Just as Sit for Greeting can be used for leashed walks, as already discussed in this chapter, it can be applied to indoor settings. I recommend putting your dog's leash on while training this behavior, even indoors. This will give you more control over your dog's body and allow you, if needed, to remove him from the entrance area if he can't handle the excitement of the incoming guest. (If you need to remove him, you can switch to the Breakfast in Bed management strategy, which safely removes him from the action.) Once your pup has practiced Sit for Greeting thoroughly and has learned how to politely greet guests, you can remove the leash.

In the early stages of training a dog to be polite around houseguests, you can combine Breakfast in Bed and Sit for Greeting. When the doorbell rings, send the dog to the bedroom or crate and give him a food-stuffed toy while your guests come in and get settled. These few minutes are likely to be quite chaotic for your excitable dog, and he may not be able to sit (yet) in the presence of these new friends. It's better to remove him than to put him in a situation in which he will fail at his training. Furthermore, it's impossible for you to train a bouncy dog to sit while simultaneously greeting guests. What is Spot doing while your back is turned and you're hugging your friend? Probably not sitting.

Once your guests have sat down and the energy is more relaxed, bring the dog out on leash, treats in hand. Now you have the attention span to focus on your dog, so training will proceed much more smoothly. With your dog on leash, approach the calmest guest first and practice Sit for Greeting as outlined earlier in this chapter. From there, take the dog to greet each guest individually. It's possible that you will need to vary your rate of reinforcement (how quickly you treat during the Sit) for

When to Call a Trainer

While jumping is generally just a rude display of goofy love, you should take it seriously. If, despite your best efforts to do positive-reinforcement training, your dog is still jumping with gusto, it's time to get feedback and suggestions from a professional. Also, if your dog's jumping involves anything that could induce pain, like biting or rough body-slamming, it should be addressed by a professional. See Chapter ❶ for guidelines to find a trainer.

each guest. While sitting to greet the calmest guest, you might treat the dog every five seconds, but you may need to increase to treating every two seconds to greet an excitable guest. If you have a guest who will get your dog super-mega-excited, it is fine not to greet that guest at all.

Once your dog has calmed down, he can have the freedom to be off-leash in the presence of your guests, provided he can be polite. If you think he'll try to climb into your great-grandmother's lap or help himself to the hors-d'oeuvres on the coffee table, put his bed or mat next to your chair and have him go to his place there. (For full Place instructions, see Chapter 3.) This way, he can be a part of the action without actually being the action in the room.

Training Strategy 2: Place

Place, discussed in detail in Chapter 3, teaches your dog to go to his mat and stay there until released. This is an effective way to have your dog do something that is incompatible with jumping; if he's sitting on his mat, he can't be jumping. This behavior takes time for some dogs to perfect, so I recommend using a management strategy like Breakfast in Bed to remove your dog from the excitement until you have practiced Place many, many times.

Place is my go-to behavior when my friends and I are having dinner or watching a movie together. In these situations, the energy level in the room is usually manageable, so your dog will be calm enough to follow your instructions and remain on his place for a long period of time. The way I see it, your dog is part of the family, and he deserves to be included in group activities. By bringing his mat into the same room where you are, he gets the satisfaction of seeing what you and your friends are doing, and you have the ability to keep an eye on him. If your dog struggles to stay on his mat, give him a long-lasting treat, like a bully stick or a food-stuffed toy. This will keep him busy for an extended length of time while he is on his mat, making it a win-win for everyone.

LEASH-WALKING PROBLEMS

Leash walking is probably the number-one frustration among owners in New York City. And it's not surprising, when every walk is a live-action video game: dodging skateboards, avoiding garbage, being ambushed by squirrels, and rushing to cross the street while the traffic light is red. There are so many things going on, your dog might not even realize you're there. The purpose of the leash-walking solutions that follow is to remind your dog that you're on the walk with him, too. Not only that, but you're even more interesting than those squirrels because you've got awesome rewards!

Loose leash walking is not the same as heeling. I reserve the Heel, with the dog on my left and his shoulder roughly in line with my hip, for short distances like crossing the street, walking past a distraction, or walking in a crowded place. (I have outlined the steps for Heel in Chapter 7.) Loose leash walking, the focus of this chapter, gives the dog freedom to choose whether he wants to be a little in front of me, next to me, or a little behind me, provided that he isn't pulling or switching sides. Loose leash walking can even include pauses to sniff, pee, or look around, as long as the dog complies when you tell him it's time to start walking again.

Everyone has her own ideas of what a typical walk should look like, but, for most people, it is a combination of loose leash walking and heeling; for me, it comprises mostly loose leash walking, with occasional heeling to get past an obstacle or through a crowded area. The rest of the time, I let my dog "do his thing" as long as he does so politely. (The guideline for polite leash walking will be laid out in detail in this chapter.) When loose leash walking, I do not demand that my dog walk behind me in some delusional display of pack leadership. In fact, I like him a little ahead of me so I know his mouth isn't full of garbage and I can watch his body language more easily. A dog walking in front of you is rarely trying to usurp your position as pack leader; in actuality, he is completely bored by your slow pace or is simply more interested in getting to the destination than you are.

At the expense of sounding like a nag, please remember that the walk is your chance to bond with your dog, not time to text your friends or run a bunch of errands (and tying your dog to a pole while you go shopping is a terrible idea for myriad reasons; see Chapter 8 for the full explanation). For the most part, you should be paying attention to your dog on the walk, and your dog should be paying attention to you. If you treat your dog like an afterthought, then expect him to do the same to you.

When it comes to greeting unfamiliar dogs on leash, I suggest you never do it. Seriously, never! It's not normal for dogs to approach each other head-on, as the sidewalk forces them to do, so by the time the dogs make contact, one or both of them could already be stressed out. Then, when the dogs try to greet, they are inhibited from saying "Hi" freely due to tight or tangled leashes, which results in more potential stress. A friendly greeting can turn into a fight, with no discernible warning to a human's eyes, caused by very subtle body-language signals.

At the other end of the misbehavior spectrum are dogs who have so much enthusiasm for making new canine friends that they become uncontrollable to walk. These dogs drag their owners down the street, head-on toward other dogs (who may be giving "leave me alone" signals left and right). They don't mind that they're choking against their collars or dislocating their owners' shoulders. Dogs like this, infinitely sweet and clueless, can start dog fights by not heeding other dogs' warning signals to back off. Moreover, since they have so much fun finding new playmates along their walks, they become consumed with a "find-the-next-doggie" game, and their owners don't stand a chance to get their dogs' attention. It's not fair to allow your dog to drag you toward every dog on the street while

expecting him to listen to you at the same time. You can't have it both ways. If your dog likes to interact with other pups, take him to supervised off-leash play groups or possibly the dog park, which is discussed in detail in Chapter 8. But while on leashed walks, channel your inner New Yorker as laid out in this chapter, and when you see another dog along your path, just keep walking.

The leash-walking problems in this chapter are divided into three sections. Distracted Doggie provides the foundation of loose leash walking. Whatever your walking problem is, this section can help, so please start here. Reactive Rascal focuses on dogs who react strongly to a certain trigger; for instance, perhaps Fiona sees a squirrel and tries to dart toward it, or Ringo barks and lunges when another dog approaches. Finally, Sidewalk Snacker gives you strategies to curb your dog's tendency to pick up all kinds of garbage on the street. It is possible that your dog falls into two or all three of these categories, so feel free to use multiple leash-walking strategies, depending on the situation.

DISTRACTED DOGGIE
PROBLEM:

My dog drags me down the street looking for squirrels, trash, other dogs, and so on. He's too interested in his surroundings to listen to me.

Management Strategy 1: Choose the Right Equipment

Would you go hiking in high heels? Or to a job interview in muddy sneakers? Let's hope not. The same holds true when walking dogs; the equipment you use can either help or hinder you. Here are the pros and cons of the most common collars, harnesses, and leashes.

Flat Collar

This is the traditional collar, usually leather or nylon with a buckle or snap, worn around the dog's neck.

Pros: For dogs who walk calmly and don't pull or lunge, this is the simplest option.

Cons: For dogs who do pull or lunge, a flat collar can put excessive pressure on the trachea and esophagus and, according to a 2006 study by Amy Pauli, DVM, et al., can exacerbate certain eye conditions by increasing intraocular pressure. As you may have already found, a typical dog doesn't seem to mind that he's choking himself while pulling against a flat collar, so the discomfort associated with pulling does nothing to teach good walking.

Flat nylon collar with a snap.

Flat leather collar with a buckle.

and keep a fast pace, it sends a message to both your dog and the other people around that you're on a mission to move forward. There's no time for sniffing, squirrel stalking, or meeting new friends. While the New Yorker walk doesn't teach your dog to be polite while on leash, it prevents him from being able to engage in bad behaviors, such as jumping, pulling, sidewalk snacking, or stopping.

Training Strategy 1: Walk with Attention

Your dog already knows how to walk; that's the easy part. The trickier part is reminding him that you're there on the walk with him. Walk with Attention is essentially an in-motion form of Check Me Out from Chapter 2, which rewards the dog for making eye contact with you. The goal of this training strategy is to teach your dog to check in with you frequently while walking, and, as a result of those check-ins, he will automatically be walking on a loose leash. Especially in the beginning, you accomplish this by rewarding the dog when he looks at you, and this reward reminds him how much more awesome you are than everything else in the outside world. With practice, you'll get a dog who is acutely aware of your presence on the walk and whose default behavior is checking in with you. Those check-ins are incompatible with sidewalk snacking, pulling, cat chasing, and so on. By simply teaching your dog to look at you frequently, you might even eliminate the need to teach him other, more complicated, leash-walking strategies.

Before the actual walking begins, however, let's talk about how to hold the leash to facilitate your training.

- Decide which side you would like your dog to be on. Have treats in your pocket or in your hand on the same side as the dog. So, if you want your dog on your right side, have the treats in your right hand or pocket. I don't care which side the dog is on, left or right. I actually teach loose leash walking on both sides because you might need to switch the dog back and forth, depending on the obstacles you encounter. Generally, my dogs are on my right side because, on city sidewalks, that keeps them to the outer edge of the sidewalk, which protects and blocks them from oncoming foot traffic. For the instructions that follow, assume the dog is on your right.
- Hold the leash, with a little slack, in the hand farther from the dog. So, if your dog is on your right side, hold the bulk of the leash in your left hand with the leash across your torso.
- This feels unnatural at first, so before you even start walking, practice indoors at a standstill. You'll notice that it's much easier to just reach down a little (or a lot, if your dog is as short as mine) to reward. If you revert to your old ways and hold the leash in your right hand (the same side as the dog) and keep the treats on the left side, you will have to reach across your body to reward. Your pup will gladly help you out by meeting you halfway, but then—whoops—you're tripping on your dog.
- Practice the following routine thoroughly while standing: Have a handful of treats or kibble. (If indoors, kibble will probably suffice.) With your dog standing or sitting to your right side, talk to him gently. Tell him how handsome he is or give him a recap of your day so far; the cheerful tone is more important than the words themselves. The moment he looks up at you, mark with "Yes!" and reward by popping a treat in his mouth from your right hand. Repeat this dozens of times. Any time he looks up at you, mark and reward

◄ Start Walk with Attention without actually walking. Jacob is standing with treats in the hand closest to Finn and the leash across his body in the other hand. Every time Jacob reaches down to give Finn a treat, it teaches Finn how rewarding it is to stay by his handler's side.

from the right hand. Then, do this activity from the left side. He is starting to learn how unbelievably awesome it is to check in with you.

Similar to Check Me Out, there is no cue for this behavior. Your cheerful chatter should be different words every time, and, as such, it is not exactly cuing the dog to look at you. For most dogs, the talking simply shows the dog you're paying attention to him, and this encourages him to look at you. However, if your dog will look up at you without the need for chatter, great! You can give him extra treats for unsolicited looks.

How to Teach Walk with Attention

Choose a quiet location to practice this at first: your living room, a hallway in your building, your backyard, an alley, or on a side street during a quiet time. You want your dog to be successful, so choose a place where he is able to focus on you and will not be overwhelmed with distractions. Upgrading to irresistible treats, like tiny pieces of chicken, deli meat, or cheese, will help him focus on you outdoors, especially in the beginning.

1. Holding the leash as previously described, walk and engage with your dog. Talk to him happily; if that doesn't get his attention, make chirping or clucking noises. There is no verbal cue for this technique, so avoid using the same word or sound each time, and avoid repeating the dog's name. You want eye contact to be a default behavior, meaning that the

dog chooses to look at you on his own without being cued every time, so engage with him naturally.

2. Any time your dog looks up at you, mark and reward from the hand that is closest to your dog. At first, do this each and every time.

3. Do your best to continue walking as you reward, though this can take some practice.

4. If you are practicing this outside, do so in short intervals, about twenty to thirty seconds at a time. The rest of the time, rely on your equipment (for example, a front-clip harness) to ensure that your dog is under control. Repeat Walk with Attention several times on each walk, at times when there are few distractions.

From there, continue to practice talking to your dog and getting his eye contact in short intervals. It doesn't have to be constant attention during the whole walk, which would be exhausting for both of you. Keep sessions short and fun. However, at the times when you're not practicing Walk with Attention, if he looks up at you without being prompted, always mark and reward in the early stages of training. What a good dog—he is choosing to be polite all on his own, even when you don't ask.

Once your dog starts to learn the game in a quiet place, he might look at you all the time. That's great! It tells you that you can start to graduate to higher levels. There are two aspects of increasing the difficulty of a behavior: (1) reducing the number of treats at the current

◀ The moment Batman looks at me, I mark "Yes!" and reward him from my right hand. Make sure to reward from the hand closest to your dog so he doesn't try to cross in front of you to get his treat.

distraction level, and (2) moving to a slightly more distracting location, for which you will go back to treating for every correct response. The following is a sample sequence, but you can adjust the process to your own situation.

- Elementary-school level: In this quiet place, once your dog has mastered Walk with Attention, slowly reduce the frequency of treat rewards and increase the enthusiastic "Good dog! You're so smart!" words of praise. Don't stop treats cold turkey. Gradually taper them off over the course of a few weeks or more.
- Middle school level: Start practicing in slightly more distracting places, like the same quiet street at a more active time or a busy street at its quietest time. When you start training in a more distracting area, go back to rewarding every time your dog looks at you. Among higher distractions, he's working much harder and needs the encouragement.
- Junior-high level: Once he is offering his eye contact in the aforementioned setting, start to slowly replace some of the treats with enthusiastic praise. Simultaneously, you can start to practice in more distracting places, like a main street at a busy time. Go back to rewarding all correct responses in this new environment.
- High school and beyond: Using this template, you can work your way up to crowded areas, like farmers' markets, train stations, or street fairs. Just remember to treat for every correct response when you start training in a new, more distracting environment.
- The final step is to phase out the treats and use mainly praise for eye contact, with two exceptions. Once a day, treat your dog for unsolicited eye contact on your walks, just to keep the game fun. (Not just any glance will do; I only reward the dog if he gives me a good, long

Scenthounds, like Beagles, can be easily distracted by tempting scents.

look. As your dog's training progresses, you'll find that he can sustain the eye contact for longer and longer.) Second, if your dog is reactive to certain things, such as a squirrel hopping by, give him a treat if he looks at you in the presence of that trigger; doing so takes a lot of self-control and is definitely worthy of a tasty reward.

- Practice with the dog on both your left and right sides. Urban dogs need to be flexible.

See the Appendix for a sample plan and chart to help you track your progress when training Walk with Attention.

Troubleshooting

Problem: My dog never looks at me. He's way too interested in the outside world.

Solution: This is a common challenge for many dogs, particularly puppies and adolescents, adult rescues unaccustomed to leash walking, and breeds that are genetically programmed to search or hunt for animals (such as scenthounds). In these cases, you will benefit from practicing indoors first, where there are no distractions with which to compete. Living rooms and hallways are suitable "preschool-level" places to get started, and you don't even need a leash to practice Walk with Attention indoors. Once you are ready to start training outdoors, reward handsomely with high-value treats when your dog does look at you, even if it's only once or twice.

Be patient with the program. Asking your dog to pay attention to you outdoors is a simple concept, but it's not always easy to execute. Also, ensure that your dog has expended enough of his energy to be able to focus. If he is relaxed after a romp at the park or a long play session indoors, that's the time to train. Asking a dog to walk politely on leash without exercising him first is like asking a child to read a book on the first day of summer vacation; it's much easier if you let the dog (or the child) burn his energy first.

Training Strategy 2: Pulling Gets You Nowhere

In addition to your dog being distracted, he may also pull. In most cases, your dog pulls because he wants to get to something fantastic up ahead, and you're just not walking fast enough for him to get there. You're going to teach him that when he pulls, he gets the opposite of what he wants, meaning that you stop and turn around, actually taking him *away* from where he wants to go. The only way to move forward is when the leash is slack. This technique is a modification of those made popular by Turid Rugaas.

How to Teach Pulling Gets You Nowhere

You do not use treats in this activity. Instead, you will reinforce polite leash walking with the "life reward" of the freedom to move forward. Rover walks nicely, and he's rewarded with the permission to keep walking, but when Rover pulls ahead, he loses his ability to move forward. The only tool you need is an iron will, because in an urban environment, it takes a lot of stopping and turning in the beginning. But I always remind my clients that if it's frustrating for you, it's even more frustrating for your dog, and therefore he will quickly figure out that a slack leash is his ticket to walking forward. Start this activity on quiet streets, at a time when you are not in a hurry. The first few sessions of this can literally be stop-and-go because you have to do this strategy every single time your dog pulls.

1. The split second the leash becomes tight, stop your motion.
2. Give the dog about three seconds to consider this. Make sure to keep your hand still and do not reel the dog in yet.
3. If he backs up and the leash becomes slack, even a little, tell him how great he is and proceed forward. Because he made the leash loose again, he is being rewarded with permission to move forward. However, if the leash is still tight after three seconds, pat your leg or use a word (not a word he knows, like "Come," but something new, like "Over here" or "This way") to encourage him to follow.
4. Turn your back and walk the other way, backtracking for a few steps, dog in tow. Tell him how brilliant he is for following you. He does not get a treat for following, just verbal encouragement.

Uh oh—Finn spots a dog up ahead.

Jacob has stopped and given Finn three seconds to slacken the leash by backing up a bit. But Finn is too focused on the other dog...

...so Jacob turns back for a few steps and encourages Finn to follow

Finn's head is back in the game, and now they can proceed.

5. Once the dog's attention is on you (usually it takes only two or three steps), turn back toward your original direction and continue on your way together. This is his reward for coming back to you.
6. As soon as you're back to your original direction, your dog may need a little help to prevent him from pulling immediately again. Practice Walk with Attention, as in the previous section, for a few steps to get your dog's head back in the game.
7. Repeat every time he pulls.

Once your dog understands this for a few sessions on quiet streets, you can venture into more exciting places. As with Walking with Attention, increase the distractions as gradually as possible. Set him up for success; don't bring your dog to Times Square and expect him to walk nicely if you've only ever practiced on a quiet cul-de-sac.

Training Strategy 3: Hand Target

Of all the behaviors I use and teach, the most useful is a Hand Target. Usually when I tell owners that we're going to teach the dog to touch his nose to their outstretched index and middle finger, I get the you-must-have-lost-your-mind look. Why would anyone want to teach that? In fact, I use hand targeting far more frequently than any other behavior, especially on leashed walks. It is easy to teach, and once your dog knows how to target, your outstretched fingers act like a magnet that can draw your dog toward you regardless of where he is or what he's doing. Skeptics might say, "If I need to bring my dog back to my side, I can just

Mind over Manners

In most cases, training a dog to be polite in an urban context is more time-consuming and requires more effort than training a dog in a quiet suburban or rural area. This is because city dogs are constantly bombarded with exciting or stressful stimuli: vehicles large and small, a constant stream of other dogs approaching, discarded chicken bones, and so on. If you feel overwhelmed when you begin training, you're not alone.

Because you can't change the bustling environment around you, the best thing to do is use it to your advantage. Rather than complain, "Oh, great, here comes another dog that Fred will want to greet," think of that approaching dog as another opportunity to practice your training. With every passing dog, your training is strengthened and your dog's behavior has one more chance to improve. It could take exponentially longer to practice this same training in a quiet area, where you only pass another dog once in a while. When you maintain a positive attitude toward training, your dog will be motivated by your enthusiasm, and you'll make progress faster.

reel him in with his leash." But try to pull your dog toward you with his leash on your next walk, and you'll see that pulling triggers your dog's opposition reflex—he will lean against the pressure and actually try to move farther away from you. A much more effective way is to show your Hand Target cue and have your dog come to you without the need for a struggle. Here are some of the ways I use it with my dogs daily:

- When I see a distraction, like another dog coming on my left, I target Beans to my right side without her resistance. Now I can do my New Yorker walk past the distraction.
- When Beans gets focused on something up ahead, I can magically reel her back in with a Hand Target so she is in a Heel position.
- If Batman puts on the brakes during the walk and refuses to move, two or three Hand Targets in a row easily get him "unstuck" and moving forward. I do the targets and reward as I walk forward, so he has to follow.
- Wednesday is garbage day, which means that both my dogs tend to have their noses to the ground. Hand Targeting in different directions—left, right, forward, backward, up, down—becomes a fun game that reminds them to look up and engage with me rather than hunt for food scraps.
- Batman, now well into his senior years, is slow to respond when I say "Come," but when I show him the Hand Target cue, he can't help but touch it with his nose.

Most dogs seem to just love bonking their noses into their owners' hands. There is something inherently cool about hand targeting for them, a coolness that is then amplified when you teach using positive reinforcement. Variations of this technique are used in canine sports, such as agility (see Chapter 8), as well as in animal-assisted therapy work that requires dogs to open doors, turn lights on, and so on.

How to Teach Hand Target

1. Rub a treat on the fingertips of your index and middle fingers and hold those fingers out at the dog's eye level, barely an inch away from his nose. Wait for your dog to notice this yummy-smelling hand and touch it with his nose. You will only make your hands stinky with a treat for the first training session.
2. The moment he touches (or crashes into!) your hand, mark and reward. Get four-for-four at about 1 inch away. He does not have to touch your two fingers exactly; any part of your hand is fine.
3. Next time, add the cue "Touch" before showing your fingers. Get another four-for-four at 1 inch away.
4. Start to add distance, an inch or two at a time. Next time, put your hand 2 inches from his nose, then 4 inches, then 6 inches. For now, keep your visual cue at eye level with the dog. Dogs tend to learn this cue quickly, so you don't need to do four-for-four at every distance unless your dog is struggling.
5. If your dog does not respond at a certain distance, go back to a slightly shorter distance and get four-for-four to make sure he clearly understands what you are asking at the easier level. For instance, your dog "touched" when your hand was 12 inches away, but when you increased to 14 inches, he simply sat and stared at you. Go back to 12 inches and get four-for-four.

B K L N

Batman loves hand targeting so much that he smashes his face into my outstretched pointer and middle fingers. This is the moment I will mark "Yes!" and reward from my other hand. Notice how my target hand is eye level with Batman.

Once your pup can easily do the Touch from a foot away, start changing the context. You can start to give the visual cue at slightly lower or higher levels, in different directions, and from increasingly longer distances so that he has to take a few steps toward you to touch. Here are some suggestions:

- Move your hand in different directions to the right and left so your dog has to make more of an effort to touch.
- Add motion by stepping away from the dog so he has to get up and follow you to touch your hand. Each time, add another step away from your dog and then cue him to touch. This essentially turns the Hand Target into Recall, and you can apply it to increasingly longer distances.
- Practice hand targeting during your leashed walks, too. Due to the distractions outside, start from Step 1 (a Touch from 1 inch away) and gradually work your way up. Once your dog can easily do Hand Targets from the full length of the leash, you can ask him to do them in the presence of a mild distraction, such as a dog barking a short distance away. (See the Reactive Rascal section later in this chapter for detailed instructions on using Hand Targets during distractions.)

Whenever you add a new variable, for example, doing a Hand Target in the presence of another dog passing by, reward handsomely. Make note of any attempts that don't work out. What made the cue too hard for the dog to perform? Too much distance between him and you?

Too many distractions? Was your voice too quiet or your hand too high to be reached?

Once your dog fully understands and responds to the cue, you can start fading out the treats. I do this by asking the dog to perform a series of two or three Touches in a row, marking each one but only treating the final one. You will probably be able to do this in a low-distraction area, like your home, fairly quickly. It might take a lot more practice for your dog to "get it" while outside.

If your dog can perform a reliable Hand Target, you will find that you are rarely pulling him (and he is rarely pulling you) on the leash. You can use the Touch cue to prevent a number of unpleasant on-leash encounters before they happen.

- You see something troubling up ahead and need to quickly turn around. Say "Touch" and show the visual cue as you change directions. Your dog turns around with you.
- Your dog is dying to pee on the neighbor's newly planted shrubs up on the left. Use a Hand Target to move your dog to your right and then body-block as you pass the tempting greenery.
- A school bus is approaching, and your dog is afraid of large, noisy vehicles. Before the bus reaches you, do a Hand Target to move your dog farther from the street side. As the bus passes, you can now body-block, using your body as a visual barrier between him and the bus.
- It's a cool fall day, and your dog has extra energy on his walk. Occasionally say "Touch" and show your visual cue as you quickly change directions. Keep him guessing by stepping in a different direction each time. This will keep his mind on you. (You can take your training a step further with the DIY agility course later in this chapter.)
- You've taken your pup to the farmers' market, and you want to prevent your dog from counter-surfing while you're paying for some items at one of the booths. Use a Hand Target to get your dog very close to your body and then ask for a Sit-Stay (discussed in Chapter 7) while you pay.

I suggest practicing a Hand Target once on each walk, every day, for your dog's entire life. Do this at times when your dog is just plodding along or slightly distracted. A surprise Touch cue breaks up the monotony of the walk and reminds your pup how much fun you are to walk with. If this behavior is part of your dog's daily repertoire, it will be easier to use it when you need to control your dog during a distraction.

Troubleshooting

Problem: My dog can't reach my hand.

Solution: In the beginning stages, remember to hold your cue hand at the dog's eye level, or even lower if necessary. Set him up for success by making it easy at first. (Bouncy dogs love to jump up to touch, but that's high-school level hand targeting, and you need to get through elementary school first.)

Hand Targeting to Get Slow Movers Unstuck

Hand Targeting doesn't just work for excitable or reactive dogs; it can be an effective strategy for couch potatoes who prefer to just sit on the sidewalk and watch the world go by. Malik Jr., the Bulldog in the training photos, falls into this category. Once he's gotten comfortable on a park bench, getting him to move can be quite a challenge. For dogs like Malik Jr., a Hand Target can get their motors running. Here is the modified Hand Target process for slow movers, which can be done either on or off leash, indoors or outdoors. This technique requires you to change your body language. Instead of facing the dog when cuing Touch, you will instead face the direction you want to go, which means you will be facing away from the dog and holding your hand out to the side to touch. This body language utilizes a dog's natural instinct to chase or follow you as you walk away.

1. Face the direction you want to go and take a few short jogging steps ahead of your dog, as if you're playfully running away.
2. As you shuffle away, excitedly cue "Touch" and show your visual cue. Continue facing forward as you jog, not looking back at your dog.
3. After he touches, mark "Yes!" and reward while you keep moving forward. This is important—don't stop your motion to feed the dog because you want to keep the momentum going.
4. As you jog ahead, do one or two more Hand Targets for a total of two or three in a row. Initially, treat each correct Touch as you continue to move. After the second or third target, your dog has the momentum to continue walking forward and has forgotten about that park bench on which he was just sitting.
5. Repeat as necessary, using an encouraging tone of voice and body language and treating sufficiently to get him excited to move forward.

Problem: My dog gets close to my hand but won't touch it.

Solution: You can adjust your body language to be more inviting. Firstly, look at your outstretched hand after you give the cue, and your dog will likely follow your gaze. If you look at the dog, then it becomes an awkward staring contest. Also, give him at least ten seconds to think it through; many dogs get confused at some point and will touch your hand if they are simply given time to ponder it. Additionally, keep your hand still as you give the cue, making sure you don't "help" your dog by pushing your fingers into his nose. If you do, your dog is essentially training you to touch his nose, and he still gets the treat! Finally, turn your body away from the dog so you are not facing him. Some dogs are sensitive to people's body language and will interpret someone's facing them head-on as "stay away" rather than "come here." Instead, turn your body to the side or actually face away from your dog and hold your cue hand out to the side rather than in front of you.

Turning or walking away, in doggie language, is an invitation to follow. I have had to use this technique with shy or fearful dogs, including my own Beans. When I adopted her, she was extremely hand-shy and hesitant to engage in any face-to-face interactions. I started teaching Hand Target by cheerfully jogging a few steps away from her to encourage her to chase me. Then, with my back still turned to her, I stopped and held out my hand to the side. This was a much less stressful encounter for her, and she felt comfortable trotting up to my side and touching my hand while the rest of my body "ignored" her. After several weeks of this, I started facing her a little more each time I cued the Hand Target. Now, she is comfortable doing a Hand Target with me, and even with many strangers, fully head-on.

Problem: My dog devours my entire hand rather than touching it with his nose.

Solution: For the first training session, I accept almost any contact, even if it is a little bitey or slobbery. However, by the second day, I start to tighten the criteria and withhold the reward for egregiously rude touches. With each training session, get pickier and pickier about which touches are acceptable, ultimately only rewarding for nose-only touches. I also will "help" the bitey dogs by pulling my hand away the second I feel contact rather than holding my hand there and allowing the dog to ingest my forearm. Imagine that your dog's nose gives you a shock, and you reflexively pull your hand away; that's what the "touch" should looks like for chompy dogs, allowing just a split second of contact.

REACTIVE RASCAL

The term *reactive* essentially means "my dog loses his mind when he sees [blank]." On a walk, when a dog seems to go wild at humans, other dogs, skateboards, or other triggers, we call that *leash reactivity*. Remember that living life on a leash is not natural to dogs. They are designed to chase small animals or herd big ones, run ahead to greet a new friend, defend their territory—and then eventually come back to you. And just because you're holding your dog back on a leash, those impulses do not go away. I can only imagine how frustrating it would be if my friend and I were walking down Fifth Avenue to enjoy a little window shopping, and every time I slowed down to peek into a shop window, my friend jerked me away and scolded me for it. Her actions wouldn't teach me to stop window shopping; rather, I would feel frustrated with her and remember not to invite her the next time I went for a stroll! So frustration about being restrained can be one cause of leash reactivity, as can fear (say, lunging at children in order to scare them and make them go away), guarding the owner, or other causes. Even the overly exuberant adolescent dog who just wants to play can become reactive when he is restrained by the leash and his excitement turns to frustration, which can look like aggression. Fortunately, while reactivity has many causes, the management and training solutions are almost always the same.

> ## When to Call a Trainer
>
> Because everyone's mental picture of polite leash walking is a bit different, only you can determine if you need professional guidance. In general, if your walks are causing you, your dog, or your neighbors stress, then something needs to change. The whole purpose of walking your dog is to enjoy the fresh air and exercise together, and if you're not achieving that goal, contact a trainer or sign up for a manners class.

PROBLEM:

My dog reacts badly when he sees people, other dogs, other animals, bicycles, and so on. (His reaction could be an excited, fearful, frustrated, or aggressive display. The solution is the same for all cases.)

Management Strategy: Choose the Right Equipment

For a dog who lunges or pulls when he sees a trigger, I generally recommend a head collar. It allows you to control the dog's head, from where the rest of his body will naturally follow. The idea is that the dog does not even try to lunge at that bicycle whizzing by, because he knows the head collar will not give him that freedom. However, as mentioned in the previous section, it can take a bit of acclimation, and the dog needs to be comfortable with the head collar in low-distraction areas first. Please also note that although the head collar is considered a safe tool, anything that gives you control of the dog's head and neck should be used with care.

I have found that, with a highly reactive dog, using a head collar can help you get the ball rolling with the training strategies in this section. I'm reminded of Mickey, a feisty terrier mix who reacted to other dogs he saw on walks. In a flat collar, Mickey normally reacted to other dogs at an intensity level of ten out of ten, complete with pulling, lunging, and frantic barking. Once he had spotted a dog and gone completely bonkers (or what trainers refer to as *over threshold*), there was nothing his owner could do. He was emotionally overwhelmed at that point. After acclimating Mickey to a head collar, the intensity of his reaction to other dogs reduced to a four out of ten, and this was before we even started training. When we did start training, he progressed quickly with few setbacks because he wasn't getting himself so worked up anymore, and, as a result, he could focus on our training much more easily.

You can certainly do the Reactive Rascal training techniques using any kind of collar or harness. Similar to a head collar, a front-clip harness can facilitate your training by reducing pulling. However, if your dog falls into the following categories, a head collar is worth trying for at least a month.

A flat collar does not help control a pulling dog.

- Your dog is reactive to triggers to the point that he could scare or hurt someone (including you) were he to get off leash.
- Your dog is strong enough to pull you or make you lose balance.
- Your dog usually notices triggers before you do (and subsequently has enough time to go bonkers before you can intervene).

For a full description of equipment, see the previous Distracted Doggie section. When in doubt, consult a trainer, because every dog's situation is unique.

Training Strategy 1: Emergency Recall

What happens when you hear your phone "ding" with a text message? Most of us feel a little rush of excitement and immediately drop whatever we're doing to check it. It doesn't matter if you're in the middle of dinner or an important meeting; you've got to check it, right? That's classical conditioning at work, and you're not so different from Pavlov's dog, who associated a bell with food. With repetition of the bell-and-food sequence, the sound of the bell triggered a similar rush of excitement and salivation. The Emergency Recall uses this principle, too, by pairing a specific sound with a super-delicious reward, so anytime your dog hears that specific word or sound, he drops whatever he is doing and thinks, *Cookie time!* Thus, he will happily trot over to you to get his treat.

Technically you're not training your dog to *do* anything (no one "trained" you to associate the sound of your text message with picking up the phone, after all), but it does require repetition for the dog to make the connection.

When working with dogs that are highly reactive, with owners whose training skills and timing are not fully developed yet, or in urban areas that are chaotic or crowded, I like to start with Emergency Recall. This is a very simple activity. You will teach the dog a unique cue that, to him, means "cookies!" It can even be the word *cookie*, though I prefer a kissy noise, whistle, or cluck, because a distracted dog might tune out your speaking voice but will definitely hear a distinct noise. Every time you use this cue, you absolutely must follow it with a great reward, regardless of what your dog is doing. Remember, we are not technically training him to do anything; rather, we are teaching him to associate the noise with a treat. (Note: Many excellent training guides discuss the differences between operant conditioning and classical conditioning, but you're in a hurry to get your dog to behave, right? So

An excited dog pulls on the leash.

we won't get into it here.) The by-product of this noise-and-treat association is that your dog will come to you.

As the name implies, Emergency Recall is a technique for getting a dog to come when he has, say, slipped out of his collar or is in a dangerous situation. I used this once for my beastly girl Beans, whose leash slipped from my grip and who darted toward the street in hot pursuit of a squirrel. One loud kissy noise from me, and Beans whirled around to come back for her treat. I think at that moment she wasn't even thinking about the treat, but the Emergency Recall response had become so ingrained (we had been practicing it daily for at least six months) that it was a reflex, like looking up if someone yells, "Watch out!"

In addition, it is also a great remedial step before embarking on Training Strategy 2. If your dog is about to react to a dog on the other side of the street, your Emergency Recall can snap him out of it and bring your dog's attention to you instead of on the trigger. This effectively prevents a confrontation and gives you an extra second or two to plan your next step.

How to Teach Emergency Recall

To prepare for teaching Emergency Recall, choose a sound (kiss, cluck, specific whistle sound, or something similar) that you do not use for anything else. You may also choose a word that you do not say often in regular conversation. From now on, this sound or word will exclusively be used for Emergency Recall and nothing else. You will also need really great treats for this; the better your reward, the more quickly your dog will be programmed to stop what he's doing and run to you. Because we are classically conditioning your dog to connect your noise to a treat, you will never phase out treats for Emergency Recall. (Going back to the analogy of a text message "ding," if you get an overwhelming number of unwanted and spam texts, you will

If your dog ever gets loose on a city street, the Emergency Recall is an essential cue.

eventually stop checking it when you hear the ding. The ding no longer predicts anything enjoyable. Likewise, if you do not always reinforce your chosen Emergency Recall noise with a treat, the noise will lose its meaning over time.) Start this sequence at home, when there are no distractions.

1. Make the unique sound you have chosen—just once!
2. Immediately give your dog that fantastic treat. It doesn't matter what the dog is doing at that moment. Don't tell him to sit or come or anything else.
3. Repeat this a bazillion or more times indoors. Casually walk around, make your unique sound, and treat.
4. Once your dog understands that your sound means "cookies," start doing it outside when there are no major distractions present.
5. Do it a few times, randomly, on each walk.

With practice, your dog should automatically come to you for his treat when you make the noise. (If he doesn't come to you, he gets the treat anyway.)

Once your dog can respond flawlessly in low-distraction areas, try it when a small distraction is present. For instance, if skateboards trigger your dog, do an Emergency Recall when a person on a skateboard is a fair distance away. Remember to always treat regardless of what the dog does; he does not have to come to you.

When your dog can consistently come to you in the presence of mild distractions, you're ready to use this technique in the presence of bigger distractions, like a skateboard whizzing past you. However—and this is important—at least once per walk, practice an Emergency Recall when there is no distraction. If you only make your kissy noise (or whatever chosen sound) in the presence of a skateboard, your dog will think the sound is warning him, "A skateboard is coming! Freak out!" In this situation, he has connected the kissy noise with the trigger rather than the treat, and he will have a negative emotional response to the kissy noise. Classical conditioning can work both for you and against you, so make sure your dog is connecting your kissy sound to awesome treats, not to other factors around you.

See the Appendix for a sample plan and chart to help you track your progress when training Emergency Recall. Keep in mind that this strategy can only get you so far. Once your dog is a little less reactive and can focus on you in the presence of a distraction, it's time to do the real work, which is desensitization and counterconditioning.

Reinforce the Recall with a treat every time.

Training Strategy 2: Desensitize and Countercondition to Triggers

Let's go back to Pavlov and his dog, who associated the bell with dinnertime and salivated simply by hearing the bell ring. That bell must have gotten the dog super-excited for dinner. Because a bell in itself is not inherently exciting, Pavlov changed the way the dog emotionally reacted to that sound by adding the consistent result of food. In the case of reactive dogs, if we take this classical conditioning a step further, we can replace the bell with the trigger that your dog reacts to.

Let's say your dog's trigger is another dog. Normally, because he feels anxious or frustrated, your dog would bark and lunge at the sight of another dog on the street, but what if that other dog predicted amazing treats? Then, with repetition, that dog would no longer produce negative feelings, but happy ones. *Oh goodie, a dog! Where's my treat?* The sight of a strange dog causes your dog to actually turn away from that trigger and look at you instead, in excited anticipation of being given a treat. This is called *counterconditioning*.

The other half of this strategy is *desensitization*. When you begin counterconditioning, you should do it when the trigger (the other dog) is far enough away that your dog is able to keep it together and not bark or lunge. We call this *under threshold*. If your dog is already barking and lunging, it is not the time to train. Imagine if someone is having a panic attack and you ask her to multiply 12 times 45. She can't do it because, while in panic mode, stress hormones are racing through her body and rational thought is temporarily suspended. The same is true for your dog; if he is over threshold, he is not able to listen to any commands, nor is he interested in your delicious treats. If your dog gets over threshold, you simply have to add distance between him and the trigger by walking away.

City folks, hold your eye-rolling for a moment. I understand that it's not always as easy as crossing the street or walking away because that street is packed with moving cars, and walking away means confronting a *different* dog that's closing in on you from behind. You simply cannot practice desensitization perfectly in all locations, so do your best. Do the counterconditioning protocol when your dog is far enough away to be under threshold. When you can't give yourself adequate distance, do your best to create a barrier between your dog and the trigger. Your dog can still learn, albeit a little more slowly, in this kind of unpredictable environment. Here are some examples of in-a-pinch barriers:

- Squeeze between two parked cars, body-blocking between your dog and the passing trigger.
- Momentarily sneak into someone's walkway or driveway, putting your body between your dog and the oncoming trigger.
- Use the Emergency Recall to bring your dog's attention to you and then treat-treat-treat generously with high-value treats while the trigger passes by.
- Make sure you're using equipment that facilitates, rather than hinders, your training. A front-clip harness or head collar acts as a built-in barrier because it doesn't give your dog the freedom to pull and lunge toward the trigger.

As your dog is progressively desensitized to a certain trigger, you will find that you can get closer and closer to that trigger with your dog remaining under threshold. The goal is always to ascertain how close you can get to the trigger without your dog feeling anxious or excited, and then you countercondition at that point. Over time, this distance will decrease, which means you will not have to cross the street or change directions forever.

Using desensitization and counterconditoning, a great many dogs learn to calmly walk right past triggers. Nevertheless, there will be days when it feels like you've taken a step backward in your training. Don't despair; this is part of the process. Your dog might have a surprisingly bad walk due to various factors; for example, your dog has extra energy because he didn't have a long walk yesterday, he feels irritable due to a sore paw, or he is exposed to too many triggers in one walk. Just take note of the circumstances surrounding that particular walk to look for causes and then see how you can improve the situation for future walks. Measure your progress on a weekly or monthly, not daily, basis.

How to Desensitize and Countercondition

1. Be ready. When you're on a walk and approaching the trigger, be prepared with a handful of amazing treats.
2. Desensitize. When you see a trigger up ahead, situate yourself so that the trigger is far enough away that your dog will notice it but not react emotionally. Urban dwellers, do your best! Cross the street (if you can) or pull over to the edge of the sidewalk well ahead of time. Note: If you cannot create enough space, it's best to turn around and avoid the confrontation.
3. Countercondition. The moment your dog notices the trigger, immediately and cheerfully say "Yes!" and treat before your dog has the chance to react inappropriately. Continue rapid-fire treating until that trigger is gone. It's critical to mark and reward before your dog starts barking or pulling. We are making the association of "I look at the trigger and get a treat," not "I bark at the trigger and get a treat." You will find it easiest to stop walking and pull over while you're counterconditioning, until you and your dog get the hang of it.

Sometimes you can't get away from the trigger and will have to manage the situation.

4. Once the trigger has passed, all treats stop and you can resume your walk. Make sure you go in a direction away from the trigger. I like to do the New Yorker walk here, just to ensure that my dog won't try to head back toward the trigger.

Going forward, you need to repeat this sequence every time you are confronted with the trigger. You will always have two choices (1) countercondition when the trigger is far enough away that your dog can stay under threshold or (2) give more space and countercondition once you are far enough away. Walk the other way to avoid confrontation if you have to.

As time goes on, you'll notice that your dog will see a trigger up ahead and turn to you as if to say, *Oh boy, it's another dog! Treats, please!* This is exactly what you want, because it means your dog has learned the "game" and is reacting to the trigger with a different kind of emotion. At this point, you can start to close the gap between you and the triggers, but do so very gradually, and let your dog dictate what his threshold is. If you push him too close to the trigger too quickly, you can undo some of your progress.

Many owners ask, "When can I start to reduce the treats when counterconditioning?" This will vary depending on the situation. As time goes on, your dog will get more comfortable with the trigger when it is at a considerable distance, such as across the street. Once he is at ease with the trigger from this distance, you can start pausing between treats. Eventually, just one or two treats, rather than the rapid-fire method from the first week, will be enough to keep your dog's attention on you. But if you encounter that same trigger in close proximity, on the same side of the street, you will likely need to rapid-fire treat. You will know if you're treating sufficiently based on your dog's behavior. A dog that can see a trigger and then focus on you is below threshold, so you can slowly reduce the number of treats. A dog that sees the trigger, gets a treat, and then turns back to the trigger and barks is not being treated quickly enough and needs a more rapid-fire approach. Here are a few suggestions for how to proceed, but your dog's progress may be faster or slower than in the following examples.

- Bella can completely focus on me when the trigger is across the street and I rapid-fire treat. Now, when I see the trigger across the street, I will reduce my treats by adding a one-second pause between each treat. However, when the trigger is approaching on the same side of the street, I will pull over between cars and rapid-fire treat.

- Bella can completely focus on me when the trigger is approaching on the same side of the street and I rapid-fire treat. Now, when I see the trigger approaching on the same side of the street, I will add a one-second pause between treats. If the trigger is on the other side of the street, it should be easier for Bella to focus on me, and I will add a three-second pause between treats.

- Bella can completely focus on me when a low-level trigger (for instance, an elderly dog) passes by on the same side of the street; I can pull over and give her just one treat. From here, rather than pull over, I will actually walk Bella past the other dog, giving her the treat just as she passes the calm trigger. However, Bella will lunge at a high-level trigger (such as a yappy puppy). In this case, I will continue to pull over and treat as frequently as needed to keep her attention.

There is no set timeline to this kind of training. I have seen some dogs respond almost

Malik Jr. gets several pieces of hot dog while Batman and I pass. Notice how Rachel has body-blocked, putting herself between Malik Jr. and the trigger. Note: For highly reactive dogs, this proximity to the trigger is too intense. Start from a distance where your dog is under threshold.

When to Contact a Trainer

Working on your dog's reactivity involves many factors, some of which you can control and others you can't. Consequently, you might see dramatic improvement right away, or it may take a few weeks to just get the timing right. Keep a journal of your progress, noting any improvements or setbacks. Also note the context of each walk, including how close the trigger was, how many triggers you encountered on that walk, if you were using new walking equipment, and so on; this will help you see patterns and prepare better for future walks. If it looks like you are seeing progress on a weekly, not daily, basis, then you're headed in the right direction. But if your progress is stagnant or the reactivity is getting more intense, you'll need extra help. In the case of reactivity, when in doubt, contact a trainer or behavior specialist using the guidelines in Chapter ❶.

immediately, while others take months. When I work with Doggie Academy clients whose dogs have leash reactivity, I tell them that counterconditioning is more like dog therapy than dog training. Whereas training usually teaches the dog to do something, such as sit or stay, therapy teaches the dog to feel something, for instance, having a positive reaction to a trigger that used to cause stress or frustration. Think of how many years a person might be in therapy before being able to regulate his or her emotions. Fortunately, dogs usually change their emotional responses to triggers much faster than humans do, but, as with any therapy, it takes time, and each patient is unique. See the Appendix for a sample plan and chart to help you track your progress when practicing desensitization and counterconditioning.

Troubleshooting

Problem: Sometimes I can't cross the street or walk the other way, so I have to face the trigger.

Solution: In this case, I will lead my dog to one side of the sidewalk or between two cars. If my dog has already noticed the trigger, I will lure him with a treat in front of his nose rather than drag him. Then I'll body-block, acting as a barrier, and rapid-fire treat until the trigger has passed. While this is not an ideal training scenario, it is effective in preventing the dog from going over threshold.

Problem: My dog is getting it, but he sees the trigger, barks once or twice, and then comes to me for a treat.

Solution: Your timing is off. The moment he sees the trigger, exclaim "Yes!" and treat before he gets to the barking part. In the early stages of counterconditioning, always be ready with a treat in your hand because sometimes you can get "ambushed" by another dog coming around a corner or a squirrel jumping in front of you. You've got to be ready to act the moment your dog sees that trigger, at least in the beginning stages of training.

Problem: I don't seem to be making any progress.

Solution: There could be many reasons for this, so contact a qualified trainer if you don't see any change after about a month. First, make sure your treats are sufficient payment for the extremely difficult work your dog is being asked to do, and make sure you are treating rapidly and consistently enough to keep your dog "in the game." I also advise tracking your progress on paper. Approximately how close can your dog be to the trigger today? What were the defining characteristics of that trigger? For example, "Bella walked past an excited Lab that was on the other side of the street. I gave her one treat every four seconds and she stayed below threshold. Then we passed a calm, old dog on the same side of the street. I gave Bella one treat every two seconds; she looked mildly agitated." Look at your progress on a weekly, not daily, basis. You will have good days and bad days, depending on all of the variables that accompany walking a dog in a city; you might even have a frustrating walk one morning followed by a fantastic one that afternoon.

Training Strategy 3: Hand Target

The Hand Target, as outlined in the previous Distracted Doggie section, is also an effective way to redirect a mildly reactive dog's focus. As with the foregoing counterconditioning strategy, hand targeting turns a situation that might stress your dog into a fun experience. It is also a good way to create distance between the trigger and your dog without having to drag him.

How to Teach Hand Target for Reactivity

The moment your dog sees a trigger but has not yet reacted to it, you will cheerfully give the Touch cue and step away from the trigger, creating a more comfortable distance. Hold out your cue hand, with index and middle finger outstretched, in the direction opposite the trigger so that your dog turns away from the trigger in order to perform the Hand Target. You can do two or three Touches in a row, if needed, and give a super reward at the end for your dog's hard work and attention. Here is an example:

1. Missy sees a cat dart in front of her and run under a car to your right. Before Missy can drag you to the right to chase the cat…

2. You cheerfully hold out your left hand and say, "Touch." This moves Missy firmly to your left side, so you can now shorten your leash and body-block if needed. Mark and reward when she touches your hand.

3. With Missy now in a more secure position to your left, continue walking forward and do two or three more Touches as you walk down the sidewalk past the cat. Keep walking as you do the Hand Targets. Each time, mark and reward.

Going forward, depending on how well Missy has practiced the Hand Target, you might not need to reward every Touch in the sequence, but rather just the last one. It could be "Touch" and "Yes!" but no treat, followed by another treatless "Touch" and "Yes!" and finally a "Touch" with a "Yes!" and a yummy treat, all the while walking forward past the cat. However, when in doubt, it's better to give Missy a treat after each correct Touch to make sure you reinforce her polite behavior of paying attention to you rather than chasing the cat. See the Appendix for a sample plan and chart to help you track your progress when training Hand Target.

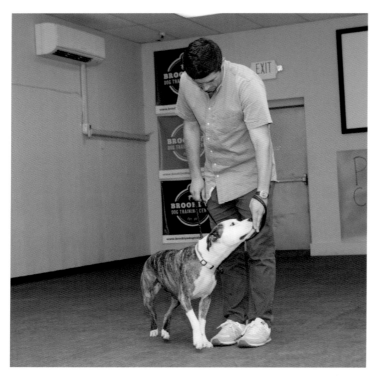

◀ As the trigger (another dog) approaches, Joe uses a Hand Target to move Susu away from it.

▼ As the trigger passes Susu, she is already engaged in the targeting. From here, Joe can body-block between Susu and the other dog.

Momo, the Tiny Fireball

Momo, the Norfolk Terrier, had two modes: mega-excited and mega-anxious. His owners Phuong and Ken did their best to expend his energy and use positive-reinforcement training, but Momo had a surplus of energy that kept him on edge most of the time, both indoors and out. While at home in their third-floor apartment, Momo relentlessly reacted to the noises of the city below by barking, pacing, and panting. This even continued through the night. On walks (if you could call them walks), Momo consistently pulled with such intensity that I thought he might be trying to take off in flight.

Problem: Momo's overlapping anxiety and excitement proved to be so intense that he couldn't focus on training. His owners' busy schedules and urban lifestyle seemed incongruous with Momo's needs.

Solution: Momo needed extra help relaxing and focusing so that his walks could be more productive and his mind would be ready for training.

- We practiced Emergency Recall, first in the apartment with success, and then in the quiet courtyard with success. Upon trying Emergency Recall on the street, Momo was too overwhelmed to even hear the kissy noise or eat the treat.
- We put Momo in a head collar so he would not be able to engage in constant pulling. Within two minutes of wearing it, Momo had relaxed and was walking down the street on a loose leash. (As they say in weight-loss commercials, "Results not typical." Most dogs take a longer to acclimate.) Now calmer, Momo could respond to the Emergency Recall on the sidewalk as well.
- Phuong and Ken enrolled Momo in doggie daycare, where he got to expend all his Norfolk Terrier energy. This had a huge impact on not only his walking but his noise-reactivity in the house. Finally, he was sleeping through the night.
- After making all of these changes, Phuong and Ken had a dog who could focus on training. They started making progress with both Walk with Attention and Hand Targeting.

Momo now has far more good days than bad days. He may always be more sensitive to noises than other dogs, and his owners are still working on his leash manners in the presence of distractions, but with consistent management and training, the future is looking a lot more peaceful for this little fireball.

SIDEWALK SNACKER

Of the many temptations your dog faces on urban streets, the dreaded chicken bone is probably the most worrisome. Many new owners have told me, "I never realized how much chicken people eat until I got a dog!" But, beyond that, edible obstacles on the sidewalk are ubiquitous, and some dogs turn each walk into a scavenger hunt for little bits of nastiness.

For sidewalk snackers, I recommend a combination of management and training strategies. The management techniques will reduce the number of opportunities your dog has to pick up tasty pieces of garbage every few feet. This, in turn, means you do not have to use the training strategies as often. But when you cannot avoid an encounter with a ripped-open garbage bag, the training strategies will give you the tools to walk past it without incident.

Since the focus of this section is on preventing sidewalk snacking, I do not include Drop It here. Drop It does not prevent the dog from picking up an object; rather, it tells the dog to spit out whatever he has in his mouth. This is also a critical skill for some snackers, and you can find a thorough description of Drop It in Chapter 7.

PROBLEM:

My dog is a like a rogue Roomba on walks. Edible or not, he eats it.

Management Strategy: Proper Equipment and the New Yorker Walk

These two management techniques, as explained in the Distracted Doggie section of this chapter, can go a long way toward stopping the snacking. First, make sure your dog is wearing a collar or harness that facilitates your training and gives you sufficient control of your dog's body. A head collar gives you much more control over your dog's head than other equipment without inflicting pain. I find that, once a dog gets accustomed to the head collar, he doesn't try to snack

The New Yorker walk is a walk with purpose.

anymore because he knows he won't actually be able to snag that chicken bone unnoticed. If you have control over what your dog's head is doing, the rest of his body is sure to follow.

For a hardcore snacker, another piece of equipment to consider is a muzzle. A muzzle is not only useful to prevent bites, but it can also prevent your dog from ingesting something dangerous. Though I generally don't use a muzzle when helping clients with their snacking dogs, consider using a muzzle if your dog has a health condition—such as food sensitivities or digestion issues—that make sidewalk

When to Call a Trainer

Asking your dog to leave garbage or to perform tricks outdoors requires a high level of impulse control on the dog's part, not to mention methodical and consistent training on your part. If you find your dog is too excited or distracted to listen, you would benefit from basic training first. Teaching your pup advanced behaviors is much easier (and enjoyable) if you've already learned how to communicate and have a solid foundation from which to build.

snacking dangerous. Additionally, if your dog is a resource guarder, meaning he might bite if you try to remove a chicken bone from his mouth, a muzzle can help you avoid a dangerous confrontation over a piece of garbage he's picked up. For owners who choose to muzzle a snacking-prone dog, it may not need to be permanent; once you have fully trained him in both Leave It and Drop It, you won't need the muzzle anymore.

If your dog's snacking situation warrants a muzzle, know that it takes some time for dogs to become comfortable with this kind of equipment, so a slow introduction is a must. It's also paramount to choose one that allows your dog to pant, drink, and take treats so you can train while on walks. Look for a basket muzzle, not a grooming muzzle, as the latter does not allow the dog to pant.

The New Yorker walk will also effectively get your dog past a delicious distraction. Kick your walk into a higher gear, and if your dog starts to slow down at the sight of that ketchup-smeared styrofoam container, briefly apply a little tension on the leash to let him know that slowing down is not an option at the moment. Keep your pace consistent and resist the urge to slow down or veer off course just because your dog wants to. I've found that many well-meaning dog owners fall into this trap: Sergeant starts to slow his walking when he spots a pizza crust up ahead, and Sergeant's handler unknowingly slows down, too. This gives Sergeant the go-ahead to slow down even more and veer toward the crust. By the time the handler realizes what's going on, it's a tug-of-war between her and the dog, both of whom end up frustrated. Here is a better way:

1. Sergeant slows his pace slightly. His handler notices this and scans the area.
2. The handler sees a pizza crust ahead. She says, "Let's go, Sergeant" and gets in New Yorker mode, accelerating her pace. "Let's go" serves to indicate that they will not be stopping. Sergeant will know that when he hears "Let's go," he won't get the chance to slow down.
3. A little later on the walk, Sergeant slows down again. His handler sees that her dog is eyeing a clean patch of grass. She says, "Go ahead, Sergeant" and gives him a little extra slack on the leash. "Go ahead" indicates that he has permission to check out the grass.

By simply adding structure to the walks, you, not your dog, will decide what he can investigate. That being said, I tell my dogs "Go ahead" a lot more than I tell them "Let's go." As long as their desired sniffing spot doesn't present a danger, I am happy to let my dogs check it out for a several seconds. (If the sniffing drags on and on, I simply say "Let's go" and start moving again.) Leashed walks are the only opportunities that many urban dogs have to interact with the outside world, and I believe it should be a time that they truly enjoy. I will never understand the ecstasy of smelling a shrub, but, to my dogs, that shrub might be the most interesting aspect of their otherwise boring day indoors. So I advocate being relatively generous with your permission to "Go ahead." However, when I say "Let's go," I mean it.

As you add these terms to your own walk, keep in mind that polite leash walking doesn't mean that your dog has to ignore every stinky fire hydrant; it simply means that when you do say "Let's go," it means your dog has no chance to investigate. Some dogs with hardcore snacking histories might need to hear "Let's go" more often than other dogs, so the balance depends on your particular pooch.

Training Strategy 1: Leave It

Leave It is the ultimate impulse-control behavior because you are asking your dog to stop approaching something that beckons him and follow you instead. It takes time and practice to build this up, but the end result is a dog that will stop in his tracks when you tell him to "Leave it" and trot back to you. While this section focuses on leaving food, you can also teach your dog to leave squirrels, skateboards, other dogs, and anything else he would otherwise head toward.

Leave It is a preventative measure that tells the dog, "Stop approaching that forbidden thing and stick with me." It is different from Drop It, which means, "Spit out what you already have in your mouth." It is easier to use Leave It to prevent the dog from approaching an object than to do damage control once the dog has gotten an object in his mouth, so I encourage you to make Leave It part of your daily practice. When you see a discarded bagel up ahead, tell your dog to "Leave it" the moment he sees it; don't wait for him to dash toward the forbidden snack. Let's put it in perspective with a human example. Like any respectable New Yorker, I love a good slice of pizza, so let's imagine I decided to cut pizza out of my diet. As I walk down the street with my friend, the smell of pizza lures me towards a shop. Before I get to the pizza shop, my friend warns, "Don't you dare go in there! You're on a diet." OK, fine. I keep walking and treat myself to a healthy snack later instead. But imagine if I go in there, buy a slice, and am taking my first bite when my friend yells, "Spit that out!" My response will likely be, "Ha, make me!" as I wolf down the slice before she can grab it out of my hands. When your dog is faced with garbage on the street, he is undergoing the same decision-making process. The most humane approach is to tell him well ahead of time that the garbage is off-limits and then reward his self-control with something even yummier. If you wait until the garbage is nearly in his mouth, it will be much harder for him to resist.

A key factor in teaching a solid Leave It is making sure that your rewards are as good as or better than what you're asking the dog to leave. Don't ask Sophie to leave a hamburger and then reward her with kibble. Rather, in the early stages, ask her to leave something relatively boring, like her kibble or a toy she doesn't care much about, and reward her with hot dogs or cheese or her absolute favorite toy. She'll start to see that leaving things is pretty awesome, and several repetitions of this sequence will actually get Sophie excited to leave objects. This excitement is critical because, with Leave It, your dog really has a choice. Being shorter and faster than the typical human, he could probably grab that street meat if he really wanted to, so we need to teach him how fantastic it is when he makes the right choice and leaves it.

There are four levels of Leave It. This kind of behavior is most successful when tackled methodically, so make sure your dog can reliably perform at the first level before proceeding to the next. Think of the levels of Leave It as school grades. Your dog has to finish elementary school (Level 1) before he is ready for middle school (Level 2), and so on. Also, resist the temptation to test your dog's Leave It skills on actual street garbage before he is fully proficient at the preceding levels. If you do use Leave It on the street before your dog is ready, he almost certainly won't leave it. That is like asking a first-grader to pass a calculus test; he's just not ready for that level of challenge yet. Set your dog up for success by practicing the following steps thoroughly before using Leave It in real-life situations.

How to Teach Leave It: Level 1

1. Sit or kneel so you're roughly at your dog's level. If your dog is sitting, that's fine, but do not ask for a Sit (or he will learn to only leave things when asked to sit first). Put some dry food or a mid-value treat in one hand. This will be the "temptation" hand, symbolizing street garbage. Your dog will never get this treat, because in real life you would never reward your dog with the street garbage. In the other hand, put an equally yummy or yummier treat. This is your "reward" hand, and you will hide it behind your back.
2. Say "Leave it" once, firmly (because in real life, it naturally comes out in a serious tone), and then immediately present your temptation treat in a loosely closed fist.
3. Stay still and quiet while your dog paws at, slobbers on, and chomps at your temptation hand. He is learning that none of these rude behaviors will get him the treat.
4. Eventually, he will give up and pause. At the moment he pauses for any reason, mark and reward from your other hand. This identifies the moment he backed off as the behavior you want.
5. Get four-for-four in that location and take a break. It may take many reps before you get four-for-four consecutive Leave Its.
6. Repeat this in several different locations until your dog is consistently backing off as soon as you tell him to "Leave it."

How to Teach Leave It: Level 2

Your body, hands, and treats are in the same position as Level 1. This time, however, your temptation hand will be open, and your dog will not be able to resist the sight of that treat.

1. Say "Leave it" and then immediately present your temptation hand, open with the treat. If your dog is facing you, hold the temptation treat off to the side as far as possible. You

◄ Beans is learning Leave It: Level 1. I said "Leave it" as I presented my fist with a "temptation" treat inside. The "reward" treat is behind my back. Now, at Step 3, I am staying still while Beans tries to sniff and lick my hand.

◣ Beans finally backs off. At this moment, I will mark "Yes!"...

▼ ...and reward her with a treat from my other hand. (Remember, the dog should never get the temptation treat.)

want to create a few feet of distance (as much as your wingspan allows) between the dog and temptation treat. Your hand should be at the dogs' eye level.

2. Your dog probably won't leave it. That's normal because we've changed the scenario. The moment he makes the slightest move forward to get the treat, snatch your hand away. He is learning that his forward motion makes the treat go away.

3. Repeat. Say "Leave it" and present the temptation treat as far away as your arm allows. Snatch the temptation treat away the split second his body moves forward.

4. After repeating this sequence a few times, he will realize this strategy is not working, and he will not move when you present the temptation treat. Immediately mark and reward.

Good dog! Don't expect him to stay still for long, though, so initially, mark after just a split second of his staying put. Reward him from your other hand. Remember not to give him the temptation treat, as it symbolizes the forbidden street garbage.

5. Get four-for-four in that location.
6. With each subsequent practice session in that location, bring your hand lower and lower to the ground. The lower your hand gets, the more impulse control it takes for your dog.
7. Repeat Steps 1–6 in numerous locations, both indoors and outdoors. By practicing Level-2 Leave Its outside, you're setting a great foundation for solid real-life Leave Its down the road.

How to Teach Leave It: Level 3

You will start this level by crouching down; by the final step, you will be standing fully erect. Because you will be tossing a treat on the ground, I recommend having the dog on leash so he doesn't simply try to outrun you for the temptation treat. The leash should be slack while practicing Leave It except if the dog darts toward the treat and you need to hold him back. In other words, when you tell your dog to "Leave it," make sure you're not restraining him on the leash. If you are holding him back by the leash, of course he's going to leave the object, but it doesn't teach him impulse control if you're doing all the work for him.)

1. While sitting or crouching, say "Leave it" and gently drop the treat on the floor a few feet away from the dog. Your dog will likely dart toward the treat, so use your hand, body, or leash to block him.
2. Just as with Level 2, repeat this until your dog learns that not approaching the temptation treat is actually what gets him the reward from your other hand. Get four-for-four.
3. Next, you will stand. When you say "Leave it" and toss the treat, toss it a little behind you at first. As your dog develops more impulse control, you can toss it closer and closer to him, but always be ready to body-block or use your leash to prevent the dog from pouncing. Get four-for-four.
4. Practice at this level in many locations, especially outside.

Level 3 of Leave It mimics real-life indoor situations, for example, if you are standing at your kitchen counter and drop some food at your feet. Your dog will be able to leave the food alone in this context. When this kind of real-life Leave It happens, remember to reward your dog with something awesome! But don't limit your practice to indoors; bring some treats outside and practice while waiting at a crosswalk, sitting on your stoop, or in any other outdoor scenario.

How to Teach Leave It: Level 4

This level is different in that we add motion. In the beginning, you will set up Leave It scenarios on your walks so you can control the outcome.

1. Prepare. Place a low-level temptation, like a paper bag or uninteresting toy, on the ground. Have a great treat ready to go in your hand.
2. Walk your dog toward the temptation, as if passing it on the sidewalk, body-blocking at first. The moment your dog spots the temptation, say "Leave it" once.
3. If your dog responds to you, mark the moment he stops approaching the temptation and continue to cheer enthusiastically for a few steps before giving him his treat. You want to

▼ Beans is learning Leave It: Level 2. I said "Leave it" as I presented the temptation treat in my open hand, a few feet away from Beans. The moment she starts to approach the temptation treat...

▲ ...I snatch it away. Beans is learning that running toward the treat actually makes it go away.

◄ Beans tries a different strategy: staying put when I say "Leave it" and start to present the temptation. (Note: Like Beans, many dogs at this stage will lie down rather than pursue the treat. That's fine. By lying down, they are leaving it!)

▼ Bingo! I mark and reward her from my other hand.

reward him once the temptation is safely behind you so your dog won't change his mind and turn back. "Leave it" now means "walk past that temptation and keep going to get your treat."

4. If your dog doesn't respond and tries to go for the temptation, just keep walking. No reward. Try again but with more distance between you and the temptation.

5. Get four-for-four correct responses in which your dog follows you rather than veers off to investigate the temptation.

6. From here, use increasingly valuable temptations, making sure that your reward is always as good as or better than what he's leaving. You could upgrade to a pile of dry food or an empty food container as a temptation. From there, a pile of training treats. Finally, actual food. Get four-for-four with each temptation.

Note: If your dog struggles with a certain temptation, it usually means one of two things. First, he needs more practice with an easier temptation. Some dogs need many reps of four-for-four at a certain level over the course of many days or weeks. Second, it could mean your rewards are not valuable enough, compared to the temptation. Make sure you reward with a treat equally or more exciting than the temptation.

After completing the previous steps, you're ready to use it in the real world. Start with rather bland temptations, which should be easy for your dog to resist. Here are some real-world Leave It examples.

- Elementary-school level: If you see a fire hydrant up ahead and you think your dog will want to sniff it, prepare for a Leave It by getting a treat ready and body-blocking. The moment your dog spots that fire hydrant, say "Leave it" and keep walking. Reward for good Leave Its.

- Junior-high level: Continue using mild temptations, such as fire hydrants, but do not body-block. This means the dog will be closer to the temptation than you are. He really has a choice here to either respond to your cue or sniff the hydrant. Be ready with a great reward when he chooses you.

- High-school level: Choose mid-level temptations, such as an empty food container or discarded bag. Body-block as you say "Leave it" and reward when he does not slow down to investigate the temptation.

- College level: Choose the same mid-level temptations, but do not body-block. The dog will now be closer to the temptation than you are. Reward generously for leaving it.

- Master's level and beyond: At this point, your dog should consider Leave It a really fun game. Once your dog looks forward to leaving mid-level items, you're ready to kick it up to food or moving distractions, such as the neighborhood cat. Continue to reward with high-value treats.

I reward the Leave It behavior long-term. Once my dog really understands how to leave things, I will use verbal praise for easy Leave Its, and I sometimes reward with a treat for leaving a chicken bone, discarded food, and the like. After a lot of practice, my dogs Batman and Beans love leaving things, and sometimes they even try to "stage" a Leave It by eyeing a piece of garbage on the street and then trotting over to me as if to say, "I didn't try to eat that garbage! Did you see?"

It's up to you if you want to reward these self-directed Leave Its with a treat or simply some enthusiastic verbal praise. See the Appendix for a sample plan and chart to help you track your progress when training Leave It.

◄ At Level 4, Jacob demonstrates what happens if you don't say "Leave it" early enough. It's too late to cue Finn to leave it now because he's already decided to go for the frisbee. At this point, Jacob can only encourage Finn to keep moving forward. Make sure to give the cue the moment your dog spots the temptation—before he gets fixated on it.

◤ Here, Jacob gives the "Leave it" cue before they reached the temptation, and Finn responds perfectly by turning his attention to Jacob.

▼ Once they pass the temptation, Jacob marks and rewards Finn. By getting his reward as they walk away, Finn learns to keep moving when told to Leave It.

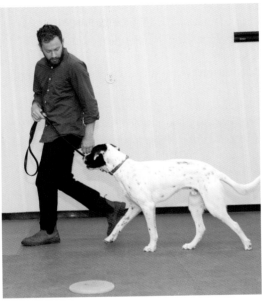

Troubleshooting

Problem: My dog seems to be on to the game. He is only leaving the temptation in order to get his reward.

Solution: This is not a problem. In fact, the goal is for your dog to think that Leave It is a game and that he is incredibly clever for learning how to ace it. If your dog performs Leave It with enthusiasm, you don't have to be as concerned about sneaky sidewalk snacking. Keep up the good work!

In this photo, the leash is being held too tightly. When practicing Leave It, make sure the leash is slack.

Problem: At levels two or three of Leave It, my dog starts to approach the temptation treat in my hand. When I then say "Leave it," he ignores me and keeps approaching the temptation treat.

Solution: Your timing is off. Make sure that you say "Leave it" just as you are presenting the temptation treat (in other words, the moment the dog spots the treat). If your dog has already taken a few steps toward the treat before you say "Leave it," you're too late because he's already made up his mind to eat the treat. Also, ensure that you remove the temptation the moment your dog starts to approach it. Don't snatch the treat away after you've already let him take a few steps and almost eat it. Just as if someone snatched a slice of pizza from under your nose, you'd feel frustrated and, from then on, Leave It would cease to be fun.

Problem: My dog will leave boring treats but not really delicious ones.

Solution: There could be a few things happening here. First, make sure your reward is equally as good as or better than the temptation treat. Also, this problem may indicate that your dog doesn't understand Leave It as well as you think. Practice each level thoroughly in many locations, especially outside, and do not ask him to leave anything that you think would be too difficult. This is one behavior that will likely take more than one round of four-for-four. The goal is to gradually and systematically work up to higher levels of temptation, just as a child gradually builds her skills from kindergarten to college without the expectation that she can skip a few grades. In your dog's case, start temptations with dry food, then move up to dry treats, then to soft treats, and finally to pieces of meat or cheese. In each case, increase the deliciousness of your rewards accordingly. You might need to practice for days or weeks at one particular level.

Training Strategy 2: DIY Agility Course

Many dogs turn to sidewalk snacking because they are bored out of their doggie minds while walking. Whereas a walk may be considered rigorous exercise for some humans, it is simply not enough to keep active dogs interested. But, not to worry—this doesn't mean you have to take up ultramarathon running or wake up at 4 a.m. to walk your dog for hours. In many cases, you can improve the quality of your walks without having to increase the quantity. How to improve the quality? Engage your dog's body and mind by asking him to perform more intense athletic activities during walks. Use common objects, like benches and fire hydrants, to turn each walk into your own personal agility adventure. You will expend more of your dog's physical and mental energy than with walking alone, giving you a dog that doesn't need to sniff for garbage in order to entertain himself.

The prerequisite for this technique is Walk with Attention from the Distracted Doggie section earlier in this chapter. First, your dog needs to realize that you're there on the walk with him. Once you have his attention, you can teach him to do all sorts of fun things.

Please keep safety in mind with all of these techniques. Depending on factors such as your dog's size, weight, conformation, and age, some of these activities might not be appropriate. I have provided less physically demanding alternative activities for the ones that follow, but I welcome you to be creative and keep your dog's particular needs in mind when designing your own DIY agility course. Here are some examples.

Target with Both Front Paws

For this behavior, your dog will put his front two paws on either a ledge or a vertical object, like a wall, tree trunk, or fence, while his back paws stay on the ground. If your dog is easily distracted outdoors, start indoors against a wall. Here is a simple way to teach it.

1. Walk up to a wall and use your palm to tap on it, encouraging your dog to put his front paws on it. The first few times, you can tap on the wall with one hand and lure with a treat with the other hand to encourage him to stand up.
2. The moment both his front paws touch the wall, mark and reward.
3. After getting four-for-four, add the word "Paws" (or the cue of your choice) right before you tap on the wall.
4. Once your dog understands the verbal and visual cues, start applying them to other upright things. The first several objects he targets should be relatively ordinary and flat, like different walls. From there, your dog can target other solid objects, such as mailboxes on street corners, fire hydrants, lampposts, and so on.

If your dog is not physically suited to standing on his hind legs, you can replace the paw target with a nose target, teaching Buddy to touch his nose to an object you point to. First, use the steps in the Distracted Doggie section of this chapter to teach Buddy the Hand Target. Then, you can transfer this targeting to other objects. Start this indoors. Say "Touch" and put your finger on a wall at the dog's eye level. Whenever Buddy touches not only your hand but also the wall, mark and reward. Practice this on several different walls or other flat vertical surfaces until he is willingly touching them, and then you can start to change the context. You'll add your new verbal cue before the "Touch" cue, so if you'd like the new cue to be "Target," you'll say "Target touch" and hold out your finger to the wall as before. This allows Buddy to hear the

The A-frame is a typical obstacle in agility competition.

B K L N

new cue first but still be able to respond to the old one. Once Buddy has figured out the game and is being rewarded for touching the wall consistently, you can drop the "Touch" part so that the cue is a pointing gesture and the word "Target."

Balance Beam

You can use elevated surfaces like benches or stairs to teach your dog to hop up, walk along the length of them, and then hop off. Benches are extra fun because they often have armrests midway along the seat that your dog can jump over. (Be careful with some wooden benches, which may have broken or widely spaced slats.)

1. Encourage your dog to jump on the bench by tapping it with your hand or luring with a treat. Walk alongside the bench next to your dog, verbally encouraging him. At the end, encourage him to jump off by patting your leg, calling him, or luring with a treat.
2. Once you're sure he's comfortable this way, add the cue "Jump up" (or any novel cue you choose) when the bench is almost in front of you and then tap or lure as before. Add the cue "Off" right before he jumps down.
3. If you are using a bench with an armrest dividing it midway, your dog can jump over it. I say "Over" before the dog jumps over the armrest.
4. Once the behavior is solid with benches, apply this process to other elevated surfaces, like the steps of a public building, where you can do several rounds of jumping up and off.

This activity assumes your dog is physically capable of and interested in jumping on and off benches. If your dog might endanger himself jumping, it's best to avoid this activity.

Circles

This one is easy for dogs of all shapes and sizes because all four paws remain on the ground. Your can teach your dog to run in a circle around any of the objects along your path: traffic

Athletic dogs can turn anything into an obstacle.

cones, light posts, street signs, hydrants, even your own body. When teaching this new behavior, practice it thoroughly in one direction first before starting the other direction.

1. Choose an object to circle, like a stool (indoors) or a fire hydrant (outdoors). It's easiest to choose an object shorter than your torso so you can reach over it as you lure and so your leash will not get wrapped around it.

2. Start by luring with a treat. Very slowly lure the dog in a counterclockwise circle to the left. It helps to use a treat that your dog can continuously chomp on as he revolves, like a piece of string cheese or a dab of peanut butter. (If you have to break it up and treat at the 180-degree point, then another treat at the end of the circle, that's fine.) For dogs who get distracted by the treat, doing a series of hand targets at 90, 180, 270, and 360 degrees is also an effective way to teach them to circle. Get four-for-four.

3. Add the cue "Left" before you lure. Practice this until your dog can go fully around the object, only getting one treat at the end of the circle. Get four-for-four.

   - For short dogs, there is an extra step here. It's likely you have been crouching down during Steps 1–3 to lure. Once your dog understands "Left" and the 360-degree lure, you can start to elevate your body. With each circle, hold your lure hand about an inch higher than the previous time. Continue to elevate your body a little bit with each rep until you are in a comfortable position. If at any point your dog doesn't respond to your lure, it means he is confused. Go back to the previous step (an inch lower) and get four-for-four at that level to ensure your dog understands that he is to follow your hand even though the treat is out of reach.

4. Do the same hand motion at the same slow speed, but with an empty hand that circles the object 360 degrees. Now your hand gesture is a cue, not a lure. Treat at the end from your other hand. Get four-for-four.

5. Gradually fade how dramatic your hand movement is. Each time, after saying "Left," make the cue a little more subtle. I do this by making the circle a little less complete with my hand each time, in extremely small increments. Rather than a full 360-degree sweeping motion, I'll do about 340 degrees and stop a little short, and then 320 degrees, and so on. The dog has to come back to the starting point (where I'm standing) to get the reward anyway. Ultimately, I'll say "Left" and point at the object with hardly any curve.

6. Follow the same sequence for "Right" to teach a clockwise circle.

If you and your dog enjoy playing these training games on your walks, check out the discussion on dog parkour in Chapter 8. You might just have a parkour dog in the making!

DOGS OF Ⓑ Ⓚ Ⓛ Ⓝ

Meet Finn

Finn, a ball-obsessed Pointer mix, was rescued from a shelter in Georgia as a puppy and transported to Northeast Animal Shelter in Salem, Massachusetts. There, tiny twelve-week-old Finn was adopted by Jacob, and he quickly started growing… and growing. At two years old, Finn is a fun-loving adult who always lets you know exactly how he's feeling, either with his booming bark or by flopping on his side when he's had enough.

Jacob's biggest training challenge with Finn was leash walking. He recalls, "As Finn grew to be bigger and bigger, I realized I needed to work on his leash-walking skills. I tried a bunch of different equipment, but the thing that has been working best is clicker training for a good Heel and stopping and changing directions when he pulls [as in Pulling Gets You Nowhere]. He's improved a ton since switching to that method."

While Finn still has his moments, namely, pulling when he gets close to the park, he's a great example of a dog whose owner identified a training problem early on and practiced every day to improve it. Now, Finn is a polite city dog and even an AKC Canine Good Citizen.

Chapter

6

N

NAUGHTY
WHEN ALONE

Wish You Were Here

A lot of dogs are an absolute pleasure to be around, but once their owners leave them alone, they turn couch cushions into piles of fluff, pee on priceless Oriental rugs, and bark so loudly that everyone in the neighborhood knows what time their owners go to work. Nobody wants to be "that" dog owner in the neighbors' eyes. A significant portion of the private clients I see are dealing with these issues, and it's not surprising, given how much time we spend away from our dogs during the day and well into the evening. While some dogs are true couch potatoes, many just aren't designed to sit in an apartment all alone for hours at a stretch.

The good news is that most of these cases have simple solutions. Though owners tend to use the term *separation anxiety* to diagnose their dogs' misbehavior, the appropriate term for many of these dogs is, quite simply, *bored*. True separation anxiety refers to a dog who cannot handle being separated from his human(s); it is a full-blown panic attack that does not subside until the dog's treasured individual returns. It doesn't matter if a friend comes over to keep your dog company while you're out, and getting a second dog won't help because what your panicked pup really wants is *you*. There is also a variation of this issue called *isolation distress*, in which the dog shows the symptoms of separation anxiety when left completely alone but is fine if left with any human or maybe even another pet. If a dog exhibiting isolation distress is left with a friend, the symptoms will subside or disappear. With full-blown separation anxiety, only the presence of you—the cherished owner—can calm his fear. Some telltale signs of separation anxiety are:

- nonstop barking or howling until you return
- panting
- drooling

- dilated pupils
- destruction near the exits (doors or windows) in an attempt to escape
- self-injury from trying to escape
- soiling indoors

On the other hand, these are behaviors that do not generally indicate separation anxiety:
- barking that lasts for several minutes after you leave, or when the dog hears a noise
- destruction of furniture or objects unrelated to the exits
- soiling indoors

You'll notice I put "soiling indoors" in both categories. While it may indicate separation anxiety, you have to rule out all other causes first. First, how housetrained is your dog? For me, *housetrained* means that Sparky has not had any accidents indoors in the last six months. This might seem like a long time, but given weather changes in temperate climates, some dogs seem housetrained until the first chilling blast of winter rolls in, and then peeing on the warm, soft carpet seems like a better option than going outside. If your dog has had accidents in the last six months while you were home (including while you're sleeping), there's a good chance you're dealing with a housetraining issue rather than anxiety.

Consider other factors, too. Have you changed Sparky's food recently or given him extra treats that could have made him drink extra water? Has he had any health issues lately or been on medication? Have you changed his walking schedule or reduced the frequency of his outdoor time? If yes, this could indicate a dog who simply had to go potty but wasn't given the opportunity. Has the weather been inclement? Has anything changed in your home lately, such as renovations or a new baby or roommate that could have thrown his routine off? Did

Damage to doors is an indication of possible separation anxiety.

Sparky come from a pet store or hoarder, was he used for puppy-mill breeding, or did he have a previous owner who didn't housetrain him? In certain cases, adult dogs who come from unsanitary conditions don't have an aversion to soiling their living spaces and might need a modified approach to housetraining. Has Sparky been punished for having accidents indoors (you know, the old "rub his nose in it" approach)? If so, he might be afraid to go potty in front of you and would prefer to hold it until you're not around.

As you can see, there are a number of considerations to rule out before labeling indoor soiling a separation-anxiety problem. On the other hand, if Sparky is only soiling in the house while alone, regardless of how many walks you took before leaving him, it may point to separation anxiety. A particular red flag is if he is having accidents while in a crate because dogs (excluding puppy-mill and hoarding survivors) typically avoid eliminating where they sleep.

A little high-tech sleuthing can help you determine whether your dog really has separation anxiety, for which I recommend seeking the help of a professional, or if he's experiencing a lesser form of distress or boredom that you can manage on your own.

1. Choose a time when you have approximately half an hour to leave the house.
2. Set up a video chat with your dog, using an application like Skype, Google Hangout, or FaceTime. You will need a computer or tablet watching Fido, and you will use your cell phone or tablet on the other end. (Alternatively, if you prefer a higher-quality spying experience, you can buy home security equipment that allows you to watch the activities in your home remotely. There are even surveillance products made especially for dogs with separation issues.)
3. Start the video chat between the computer and phone while you're still at home. Put your cell phone on mute so that you can hear your dog, but he can't hear you.

Destroying furniture could be more about boredom than separation anxiety.

4. Take yourself and your phone out for coffee while watching what Fido does when he's alone. Give him a solid thirty minutes of alone time to see if he falls into the "separation anxiety" or "bored" category. If it is the former, the following strategies will help, but you should also enlist the help of a trainer or behavior specialist to develop a personalized plan to alleviate his anxiety. If your dog falls more into the "bored" category, use whichever of the following strategies fit into your lifestyle.

PROBLEM:

My dog barks and/or destroys things when I leave the house.

Management Strategy 1: Engage the Mind

When you leave Sparky alone, he's left to make his own entertainment. Have you ever seen those home videos of a dog waiting for his owner to leave and then hoisting himself up on the kitchen counter to fix himself a snack (or twelve)? I imagine that dog is experiencing the opposite of separation anxiety; he probably couldn't wait to be alone! However, there are plenty of dogs out there who do get mildly anxious when their owners leave, and the worst part is usually the first few minutes of being alone. Engaging the dog's mind during this time with an appropriate toy or game helps alleviate the stress of seeing his owner go.

Here, the pet-toy industry has got you covered. One visit to a pet-supply store, and you'll be dazzled by the number of interactive toys for dogs. Easy ones, hard ones, big ones, small ones, treat-dispensing ones, ones for heavy chewers—you get the idea. I suggest getting several different toys and rotating them so your dog doesn't get bored. Focus on toys that you can stuff with food or treats because they will hold a lonely dog's interest much better than a run-of-the-mill rope toy or ball. When you're home, store the special toys out of reach to create a sense of excitement when your dog sees you pull them out next time. I've used this strategy successfully with both of my dogs, Batman and Beans. I keep two peanut-butter-stuffed durable toys in the freezer, frozen and ready to go. (Frozen peanut butter requires greater effort and time to eat than room-temperature peanut butter, thus keeping the dog entertained for longer and making him expend more energy to get the goodies out.) When I pull out the frozen toys, both dogs get the "kids on Christmas morning" look of excitement and anticipation. I can tell that while I'm tying my shoes and putting on my jacket, all they're thinking is, *Will you leave already? We want that peanut butter!* I'm pretty sure that my departure is the best part of their day, and that's fine with me.

Some engaging toys worth checking out include:

- hollow toys, such as the various Kong products, which you can fill with the dog's dry and/or wet food, peanut butter, plain yogurt, cream cheese, or meat baby food (for human babies, that is)
- High-tech treat-dispensing toys, such as Treat & Train or Puppod, that owners can control remotely
- puzzle toys, such as those by Nina Otttosson, in which kibble or treats are hidden in various compartments and the dog must figure out how to get the food
- a snuffle mat, which resembles a square of shag carpet on which you sprinkle kibble or treats for your dog to find

Keep your dog's safety and needs in mind when looking for an appropriate toy. Some might be too hard or too soft or present a choking hazard to certain dogs. You usually can't go wrong with a Kong Classic, as it comes in different strengths and sizes. I recommend buying them two sizes bigger than your dog's actual size. My dogs are small, at roughly 10 pounds each, and I use the medium size for their frozen peanut butter snacks and the large size to feed their meals.

I don't recommend the following:
- toys small enough to be accidentally swallowed
- toys with small parts that could be chewed off and eaten
- toys that could roll under furniture, which could lead to frustration barking
- chewies like rawhide, bully sticks, or antlers, which can pose choking hazards

Once you've chosen an appropriate toy to engage your dog's mind, your departure will look something like this:
1. Right before you leave the house, pull out your treat-dispensing toy.
2. Bring the toy where you would like your dog to be, such as in a certain room or in his crate. Ask him to sit politely.
3. Once he is sitting, he can have his treat. Now, quietly leave without any tearful good-byes or other drama.

A Word about Rawhide

While I am not opposed to rawhide as an occasional treat (and an indispensable tool to occupy teething puppies and play-bitey adolescents), I use it with caution and only under human supervision. Rawhide is generally safe if the dog chews it until it is soft, at which point the dog can tear off that soft piece and swallow it. To reduce the risk of choking, I always buy rawhide that is one or two sizes bigger than recommended for my dog's actual size. This means he will not be able to easily tear off a hard piece and swallow it. I also throw out the rawhide once it gets down to a hard nub that my dog could swallow whole before chewing it to soften it. (When taking rawhide away from my dog, I always give him a treat in exchange so he doesn't learn to guard his rawhides from me.)

Be picky about which rawhide you buy. If I don't see the country of manufacture proudly advertised on the label, I am automatically suspicious of that rawhide's origins and safety. Also, rawhide chews made of one single piece are less of a choking hazard than those made of many pieces pressed together.

I should mention that there are some dogs who aren't good candidates for rawhide or bully sticks, including dogs who inhale their food without chewing and dogs with resource-guarding tendencies. While I am selective about my rawhides and bully sticks, I never give my dogs antlers because several veterinarians have found them to be so hard that they could crack dogs' teeth.

Management Strategy 2: Engage the Body

It's unfair to expect a dog to be calm while home alone if he hasn't had the opportunity to expend all of his energy beforehand. In many cases, we underestimate how much exercise our dogs really need; a walk around the block is not nearly enough to satisfy some dogs. Imagine going to your favorite Italian restaurant and, when your pasta dish comes, it has three little strings of spaghetti and one microscopic meatball. You'd be thinking, *That's delicious, but I want more*, and you'd be left feeling unsatisfied. That's how your dog feels when you take him on a short walk. He wants more, and if he can't drain his energy outdoors, he'll do it by reupholstering your furniture.

Yes, giving your pup enough exercise takes time, but it is time well spent if your dog is too pooped to chew off your crown molding while you're at work. You have some options:

- Take a long walk or, even better, a jog with your dog before you leave for the day.
- If your time is limited, create a DIY agility course as outlined in Chapter 5. You can even do similar exercises indoors when the weather is bad.
- Take different routes as much as your neighborhood allows so that your dog gets to see, hear, and smell new things, all of which can help burn a little extra energy and reduce boredom.
- If your dog loves to romp with doggie friends or play fetch with you, a morning trip to the dog park gives him the chance to blow off steam while you enjoy your coffee. (See Chapter 8 for a discussion on dog parks.)
- Hire help to exercise your dog. This is discussed in Management Strategy 5, later in this chapter.
- Get involved in a sport like agility or dog parkour, as described in Chapter 8. You don't have to practice the sport every day to see behavioral benefits.

Management Strategy 3: Confine to a Safe Area

Don't feel badly leaving your dog in one room or a crate while you're out; your dog may actually be more comfortable that way. Having access to the full apartment or house stresses some dogs out and keeps them on alert, just as having too many responsibilities at your job can stress you out. In my apartment, we jokingly refer to the living room as "the panic room" because that's where our dogs are safely confined when home alone. It's a comfortable and cozy room with plentiful sunbeams, dog beds, and an air conditioner, and the dogs can see the front door but don't have direct access to it. Similarly, if your dog is crated, I recommend keeping the crate where he can see the comings and goings of the family; for example, in a quiet corner of the living room.

For dogs with a history of barking at noises outside the door, it's a good idea to block access to the front door, either by crating the dog or by putting up a gate or fence. Once the dog isn't faced with the responsibility of guarding the door, he automatically settles down. I generally avoid leaving a dog alone in a more removed area, such as a bedroom, home office, or bathroom, because some dogs' stress increases when they are so far from the action. If you do choose to use a more removed room, a gate will be a less stressful barrier than a closed door.

A crate-trained dog can be comfortable in his crate when left alone.

If your dog isn't responsible enough to handle free access to a room, crating is generally your best option. When properly crate-trained, your dog will find it a safe, comfortable place and will choose to relax in there without being asked. If your dog can handle having his favorite bed or blanket in the crate without destroying it, that will sweeten the deal; however, if he shreds his belongings, then remove them from the crate until his crate training is complete or he has entered a more mature life stage. (Dogs have lived for tens of thousands of years without dog beds, so he'll be fine.) A crate should be large enough for your dog to comfortably stand up, lie down, and turn around. If your dog is still growing, you can purchase a larger crate that will fit him as an adult and then use a divider (sold with the crate) to adjust the size of the crate as he grows. A crate that is too large can allow a yet-to-be-housetrained dog to use one corner as a toilet and the rest as sleeping space, so bigger is not always better.

How to Crate-Train

Crate-training should begin well before you actually have to leave your dog in the crate unattended. The whole idea is that you don't push the dog beyond his comfort level because that can create a negative association with the crate. Whenever I put a dog in his crate, I use a hollow toy filled with his meal or other goodies, like peanut butter or plain yogurt.

The following steps describe the "fast track" to crate-training. This is only appropriate for dogs who seem perfectly comfortable with being locked inside the crate. If your dog becomes uncomfortable at any point, switch to the "slow and steady" steps that follow the fast track. How do you know if he is uncomfortable? A dog who barks, whines, pants, or scratches while in the crate is telling you that he's stressed and needs a slower approach.

From Country Bumpkin to City Slicker

The majority of New Yorkers I know are actually transplants from the suburbs or countryside. And the same goes for our dogs. Approximately half of the dogs in my manners classes are rescue dogs transported to the city from rural shelters in the South, where the euthanasia rates are extraordinarily high, and even the cutest of puppies don't stand much of a chance. My Chihuahua/terrier mix, Beans, rescued from South Carolina and transported to Our Best Friends Rescue on Long Island, New York, is among the lucky ones who got a second chance.

If you have brought a dog, particularly an adult dog, from a rural area into your city home, be patient. It can take several months for a dog to get fully acclimated to his bustling new life, and, during that time, his stress can cause him to exhibit "bad" behavior. Remember that your new dog has probably been through one or more shelters, on a transport van, and in a foster home before settling in with you, and he is likely confused and overwhelmed. Many rural rescue dogs have never been on a leash or lived indoors before, and it's likely they have not had any training. Therefore, new rescues might bark or destroy items while left home alone, which is why I recommend management strategies, especially in the first few months. In almost all cases, with a little time and consistent practice of the techniques in this book, these unwanted behaviors will subside or disappear entirely.

Let's face it: the first few weeks with a new dog, rescued or not, are stressful for everyone. In my family, we joke about our "buyer's remorse" after bringing home a new dog because at first it feels more like having a strange roommate than a canine family member. But, as time passes, there is nothing more satisfying than adopting a dog and watching him learn to trust and communicate with his new family more and more each day. As the photo shows, Beans has acclimated to city life and doesn't see a darn thing wrong with being an urban dog.

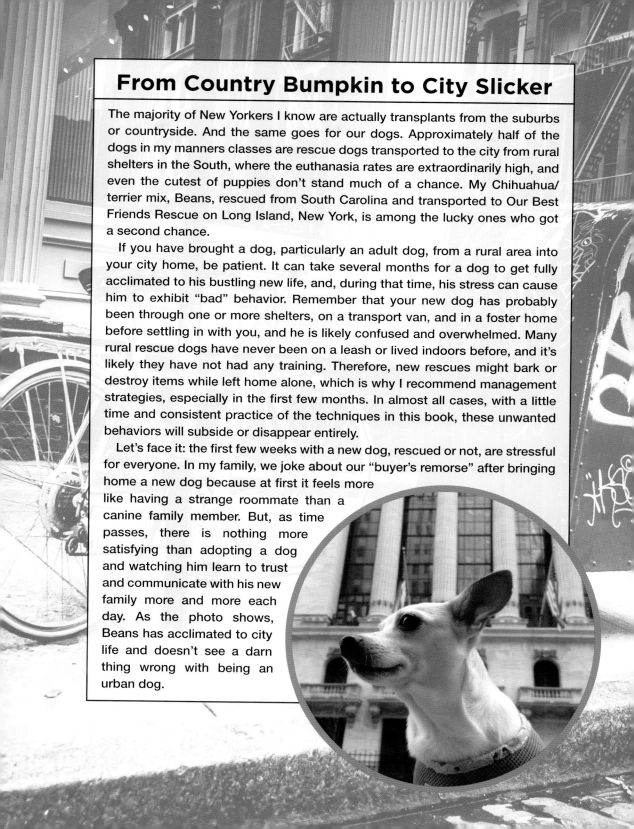

1. Feed your dog his meal stuffed into a toy in his crate. Put the toy in the back of the crate and let your dog enter on his own, without coercion. Shut and lock the crate door after he enters the crate. Walk away but keep an eye on your dog for signs of stress. When he has finished his meal, immediately let him out.
2. Practice Step 1 for several meals to ensure he is comfortable. Once your dog will comfortably go into the crate, add the verbal cue "Crate" before putting the toy in the crate.
3. Say "Crate" and feed the meal in the locked crate as before. When he has finished his meal, leave him in the crate for another minute. Assuming he is not barking or scratching, let him out. (If he is barking or scratching, see below.)
4. Each time, increase the length of time your dog is in his crate, minute by minute. While he is in the crate, go about your business and leave him alone in the room at least part of the time. Assuming the dog is not barking or scratching, let him out.
5. Use the "Crate" cue and toss a treat or stuffed toy into the crate at times other than mealtimes. Leave him in the crate for different lengths of time—sometimes one minute, sometimes ten minutes.
6. Use the "Crate" cue but withhold the treat until the dog has entered the crate. Once he enters, he can have the treat or stuffed toy as you shut the crate door. Leave him in the crate for a variable amount of time, as in Step 5.

If your dog shows signs of stress, take the following "slow and steady" approach. The goal is to make crate-training fun, not stressful or overwhelming.

1. Feed your dog all of his meals inside the crate with the door open. At first, you might have to put the food-stuffed toy near the front of the crate and then push it a little farther back with each meal. Walk away while he is eating. Repeat until he is comfortable eating in the crate.
2. Feed your dog in the crate as before, but gently swing the crate door open and closed several times while he eats. Sometimes, close and lock the door for several seconds and then open it again. You are conditioning him to the sound of the door and to very short periods of confinement.

3. Once he is comfortable with Step 2, add the verbal cue "Crate" right before you put his meal in the crate. As he's eating, close and lock the door for the duration of the meal. Walk away while he's eating. Release him when he's finished eating, before he starts to whine. We are teaching him that having the door closed is no big deal.

4. Now, say "Crate," feed him in the crate, close and lock the door, and walk away. After he has finished his meal, leave him in the crate for one minute. Again, the idea is to show him that it's no big deal.

5. Once your dog is fully at ease with this sequence, say "Crate" but do not give him the meal yet. Wait for him to go into the crate himself. Once he chooses to enter the crate, give him the meal and continue with the sequence as before.

6. Gradually prolong the amount of time he's in the crate, about one minute longer for each meal. Stay out of sight while he's in the crate. If this progress is too fast and causes barking or whining, you can increase his confinement time by only a few more seconds with every meal. Let your dog dictate the pace of his progress.

7. At random times throughout the day, cue "Crate" and give the dog a different goodie, like a treat, toy, or chewy. Leave him in the crate for varying lengths of time: sometimes, one minute; other times, ten minutes. Practice this as much as possible.

8. Now you can use "Crate" in other contexts, like when you're taking a shower or when the plumber comes to fix your sink. Give your dog something fun to do while he's in the crate, such as a treat-dispensing toy or a rawhide (if supervised).

Even with the slow and steady approach, you might need an intermediate step if your dog appears suspicious of the crate. For instance, between Steps 1 and 2, you could add a step in which you feed him in the crate, swing the door closed only once while he's eating, and immediately open it again. The goal is to keep your dog in the crate for a length of time that is tolerable and stress-free for him. The tricky part is this: if he starts to whine or cry while locked in the crate, do not let him out. This will only teach him to whine and cry and thrash until someone comes to rescue him.

Rather, wait until he has quieted down, teaching him that only polite, quiet dogs will be let out. The reason I say it's tricky is because there are two exceptions: (1) if your dog has to go potty, you should let him out immediately; and (2) if your dog has true separation anxiety, he will not stop crying and could even escalate to injuring himself in an attempt to escape the crate. In the latter case, contact a trainer for help.

While crates are excellent management tools, a dog should be crated only for a limited time. A puppy should not be crated for longer periods of time than he can "hold it" (unless he is confined in an exercise pen with a wee-wee pad), and even an adult dog should get the opportunity to stretch his legs every three or four hours. A dog should not be crated all day while you're at work and also frequently crated while you're at home to keep him out of trouble. Constant crating will likely exacerbate his behavioral problems because he has no outlet for his energy and can become frustrated from extreme cabin fever. If you find yourself crating your dog for more than a few hours a day, there are professionals who can help, including trainers who can show you how to improve your dog's manners. There are also dog walkers and doggie-daycare facilities that specialize in giving dogs safe outlets for their energy. See Chapter 1 for instructions on finding a trainer, and Management Strategy 5 in this chapter for dog walker and daycare considerations.

Management Strategy 4: Create a Doggie Spa at Home

File this one under "can't hurt, might help." While these techniques alone are unlikely to cure full-blown separation anxiety, they encourage your dog to relax and can be paired with the other strategies in this chapter. If you think creating a spa-like atmosphere seems silly, consider this: do you think more people have meltdowns at the DMV or at a spa? While it's certainly possible to lose your cool at the spa, there's something about the soothing music, calm staff, and earthy tones that naturally relax even the most neurotic New Yorkers.

For the benefit of my human and canine family members, I've taken steps to make at least my living room, where the dogs and I usually spend time, as relaxing as possible. These are some considerations for creating a calm atmosphere, based on what's worked for me personally and what Doggie Academy clients have found successful:

- Favorite bed or blanket. Bring your dog's favorite bed, blanket, or toy to the area where he will be confined when alone. This assumes your dog will not destroy it. Some dogs take great comfort in a familiar item and will feel more secure with it. For dogs that love their crates, the crate can also have a calming effect. My senior dog, Batman, is very attached to a particular blanket (or what's left of it); he's slept with it every night since I adopted him more than a decade ago. I remember one time, when my husband and I took a vacation with the dogs. In the hotel room, I pulled Batman's blanket from my suitcase. While it was still dangling from my hand, he leapt up into the blanket and immediately entangled his whole body in his prized possession, snorting with pure joy. Partially thanks to that blanket, I knew I could comfortably leave Batman in the hotel room while we went out to dinner that night.

- Soothing music. Like some animal shelters and hospitals, I play classical or spa music at home for its calming effects. You can find countless choices on free streaming websites, and there are even compilations made specifically for dogs. I recommend playing the music sometimes while you're at home, not just when you leave. If you exclusively turn it on before you leave, the music can actually be a trigger that means, *Oh no, I'm going to be home alone soon*, causing stress. But if you also play the music while you're hanging out in the room or doing chores around the house, your dog will not make any particular association with it. Interestingly, when I play calming music in my living room, I find that my dogs come in and promptly fall asleep. Is it a coincidence? You'll have to ask them.
- White noise near the door or window. In addition to or instead of calming music, consider soft white noise, like the noise of a fan. (You can also find free white noise on websites such as YouTube.) When I leave my apartment, I turn on white noise near the front door, so even if my dogs hang out in the foyer, they can't clearly hear neighbors passing by. If they can't hear it, they won't react to it.
- Doggie massages. A short daily massage using slow, long strokes is a great way to keep your dog's stress level low in general. My girl Beans loves a technique called Tellington TTouch, which is similar to massage and has helped calm her in stressful situations, like train rides.
- Flower power. Aromatherapy can have a relaxing effect on humans and animals. You can add a single drop to a diffuser, which will fill the room with the subtle smell of lavender, lemon, or whatever aroma you like. (One drop is anything but subtle to the sensitive nose of a dog.) Furthermore, tinctures like Bach Rescue Remedy, when added to your dog's water or food or rubbed on the ears or paws, have also been documented to calm some animals.
- Pheromones. Some owners have found dog-appeasing pheromones (DAP) to help ease their dogs' various anxieties around the house. This product, which is sold as a plug-in diffuser and in other forms, releases pheromones similar to those of a dog nursing her puppies, which has a calming effect.

Management Strategy 5: Hire Help

If you live in a city, there's a good chance you can find a reputable doggie daycare facility or dog walker to help you tire your pup out. A good doggie daycae or dog walker is an invaluable investment in your dog's physical and mental health, and they can give you peace of mind when your health or work schedule limits your ability to exercise your dog. Let's look at both options.

Doggie Daycare

How It Works

Doggie daycare is a relatively new concept, and the facilities you'll find will run the gamut. In most cases, urban daycare centers include one or more open indoor areas for dogs to play; there may also be an area with crates and an outdoor area, depending on the facility. For safety, there should be separate areas for large and small dogs. The facility should take all precautions against predatory drift, in which a small dog suddenly triggers the predatory instinct of a larger one and becomes prey. Therefore, if your dog is small, make sure the large dogs can't access or jump into the area for the little ones. As far as scheduling daycare visits, many facilities offer half-day or full-day options. If your schedule allows, consider a half day because eight or more hours of canine play per day can be exhausting to some dogs. Like overtired babies, overtired dogs can get cranky.

Dogs Who Would Benefit

First and foremost, daycare is meant for dogs who enjoy the company and play of other dogs. It is not meant to "teach" your unsocialized dog to be friendly. Consequently, daycare may not be right for all dogs, just like team sports aren't suitable for all humans. If your dog doesn't enjoy daycare or is rejected by a facility after the behavior assessment, it doesn't mean there is something wrong with him; it simply means that there are other activities, like playing fetch in the park or taking agility classes, that better suit your dog's personality.

A dog's energy level is another consideration. If your dog seems to have infinite energy, even after a long walk or jog, then daycare will probably give you more bang for your buck than a midday dog walker. If your dog is having a blast at daycare every day (or even once or twice a week), you're not under pressure to hurry home after work to expend all of your dog's pent-up energy. I've had clients say that daycare saved their sanity because, at the end of the day, everyone was equally tired and both humans and dogs could relax on the couch together.

Finally, if your dog suffers from separation anxiety (or simply is destructive or constantly barking while alone), daycare indirectly manages this problem.

Things to Look For in a Daycare

Be picky and do your homework before choosing a daycare facility. Because doggie daycare is a relatively new and unregulated field, you will find huge variations in quality and standards. Find answers to the following questions before signing your dog up.

- Does the facility assess sociability and behavior before accepting a dog? It should. How many dogs with behavior issues are accepted, and how are those dogs monitored? Under what circumstances would a dog not be invited back to the facility? While no one wants his or her dog to be kicked out of daycare, for safety reasons, the facility should enforce strict policies related to dangerous behavior.
- What training does the staff receive? Refereeing dogs requires knowledge of dog play style and body language, quick responses, and familiarity with safety procedures, such as breaking up a fight. Employees need to be trained accordingly. A daycare whose employees have had formal training and are certified in pet first aid would be at the top of my list.
- How does the daycare separate dogs? Do not even consider one that puts dogs of all sizes together or uses a flimsy fence to separate them.
- Does the facility use crates, and under what circumstances? Crating is fine for short periods, but you're paying for your dog to be getting some exercise and expending some energy.
- How does staff clean the facility? Due to limited urban space, the dogs might just have to use the indoor space to potty, which is not the end of the world as long as someone is monitoring the indoor potty space and cleaning it immediately after any of the dogs use it. (Actually, I would prefer my dog to use the open floor to potty rather than take a walk down the street with a staff member, where he could escape or pick up chicken bones.)
- How many dogs are there per square foot? How many dogs are allowed to play at one time? What is the staff-to-dog ratio? A reputable facility will know all of these numbers; the lower the ratio, the better.
- What associations does the facility or its staff belong to? While daycare is currently unregulated, membership in pet care associations at least shows a commitment to paying annual dues.
- Does the staff train dogs, too? If so, using what methods? Since anyone can call herself a trainer, the individual's qualifications should meet the criteria listed for trainers in Chapter 1. Training is a completely different field with separate qualifications, and anyone training your dog would need to do so separately from group play.

Dog Walkers

How it Works

As with daycare, there is a great deal of variety among dog walkers: their schedules, prices, qualifications, and so on. The right dog walker can put your mind at ease while you're at work because you'll know that your dog is getting a break from the monotony of being home alone. A dog walker will come to your home during a predetermined window of time to give your dog a walk and a little attention. He or she usually can also administer medications or feed your dog, possibly for an additional fee.

For dogs that only need a "pee break," walkers generally offer twenty- or thirty-minute visits. For dogs with more energy to burn, walkers may offer hour-long walks or even jogs. You might be able to get a lower price if you do a group walk, consisting of your dog and a few other dogs from the neighborhood. A group walk is just that—a walk—so don't expect doggie playtime. If you've ever seen the dog walkers in Manhattan, taking up the entire sidewalk with packs of a dozen leashed dogs of all shapes and sizes, you know that these folks are on a mission and do not stop at every hydrant. (I don't actually recommend a pack walk that large, since even the best walker with the most amazing peripheral vision can't watch that many dogs at once. What if one got loose? How would that walker get the dog back?) Regardless of the kind of walk, a good walker will follow up with a note or e-mail after each walk to tell you how it went.

Dogs Who Would Benefit from a Dog Walker

Dogs who are generally comfortable home alone, medium- to low-energy dogs, or high-energy dogs who aren't suitable for daycare would do best with a walker. After adolescence, your dog may actually prefer to lounge quietly at home instead of being bombarded for hours on end by younger dogs. If your dog is skittish or easily overwhelmed, he could benefit from the one-on-one relationship that develops with a walker. I remember when I first brought Beans into

Although this is a common sight in New York City, your dog will fare better in a smaller group or one-on-one with the dog walker.

our home; having come from a hoarding situation with presumably no contact from outsiders, she was extremely anxious around new people. We specifically hired a calm walker to come over, at first while I was home, just to spend time with Beans. After a few sessions, Beans trusted her dog walker enough to venture outside with her. Now we're past needing such gradual introductions to all people, but, in the beginning, the patience and flexibility of our dog walker was very helpful.

Things to Look For in a Dog Walker

Like daycare facilities and dog training, dog walking is an unregulated business. Do your homework and find out these details about a dog-walking business or individual walker:

- How many walkers do they employ, and who will visit my dog? There are some large dog-walking companies with numerous staff members. They can likely accommodate last-minute appointments or additional needs, such as dog sitting, but they may rely on more than one staff member to provide service to your dog. Are you and your dog comfortable with different walkers coming into your home? On the other hand, smaller companies might ensure the same walker each time, but you are limited to that individual's schedule and circumstances.
- What kind of training or experience does the walker have? Take a look at the business's website. Do they talk about how much they love dogs or how experienced they are in handling dogs? Being a dog lover is different from being a dog professional. She doesn't necessarily need formal training (though it would be wonderful), but she should have experience with pets other than her own. If your dog walker says that she can also train your dog, hold her to the same criteria to which you would hold any trainer (see Chapter 1). Exercise caution if your dog walker flippantly claims to be able to correct problem behaviors, as this requires high-level training experience, a consultation with you, a thorough understanding of your dog's background, and other considerations.
- Does the walker text or wear headphones while walking? This is unacceptable. Your dog walker should be paying attention to your dog to make sure he's not ingesting chicken bones or about to chase a squirrel into traffic.
- What associations does the business belong to? These associations do not evaluate the quality of the business, but they do show a certain level of commitment. The company should also be bonded and insured. If your designated walker has any certifications or educational background in dog behavior or first aid/CPR, that's a big plus.
- If doing a group walk, how many dogs will be walked with yours? Group walks can be more cost-effective and, for some dogs, more enjoyable; however, they have more inherent risks

than solo walks. Dogs who walk together should be sociable and relatively easy to handle, which is important because the walker's attention will be divided among a few dogs. If your dog is leash-reactive or overly exuberant, he would be better suited to a one-on-one walk. Even for calm dogs, consider how many dogs will be walked together and how often those pairings will change. Generally speaking, the smaller and more consistent the group, the better. Finally, ask your walker where she will secure your dog while she picks up or drops off the other one(s). The dogs should always be left in a safe place; in a city, this generally means inside the building or apartment. Leaving the dogs unattended outside is a disaster waiting to happen.

Training Strategy 1: Teach a "Find It" Game

This simple game is a great way to change how your dog feels about being left alone. He'll learn that, once you leave, the scavenger hunt begins. It takes only a little training initially, and in no time your dog can play the game without you being present. When I play this game at home, I save a portion of my dogs' dinners for the game (you can play this in a multiple-dog household, provided that you don't have a resource guarder among them). We play Find It not only when I leave the apartment but also when we're cooped up inside on rainy or snowy days.

How to Teach Find It

1. Let the dog sniff a treat in your closed hand so he knows what to look for. Then say "Find it" and toss the treat in plain sight.
2. Your dog eats the treat, and you cheer. *What fun*, he thinks to himself.
3. Get four-for-four.
4. Now hide the treat while your dog watches and then say "Find it."
   You can hide it in an easy place, like behind a table leg.
   - If your dog is rushing to the treat, put him on leash. Hold or step on the leash while you stretch to place the treat. Alternatively, if your dog knows a Place or Sit-Stay, this is an excellent way to practice those skills in a real-life context.
5. Get four-for-four.
6. Next, bring him into another room and either shut the door or ask for a Sit-Stay so he can't see you hiding the treat. Hide the treat in an easy spot, in plain sight, on the floor.
7. Release him from the Sit-Stay or open the door and say "Find it." Let him look and sniff around for the treat. He might need a little help in the beginning, so it's OK if you look or point toward the treat the first time. After that, I don't look or point because the dog needs to develop independence here; however, I might say "Nope" in a flat tone if the dog is in the totally wrong area or

Glamorous, Clamorous Clare

Clare, a senior Beagle mix with an irresistible charm, hit the jackpot when she was adopted by JoAnne, an apartment-dweller in Brooklyn. As with many rescues, Clare's journey home had many stops: from unknown origins to a rural southern shelter to a transport van and ultimately to Sean Casey Animal Rescue, a no-kill shelter in Brooklyn. When JoAnne adopted her, she found that Clare had a lot to learn about indoor living, particularly about being left alone.

Problem: Clare was showing signs of distress when left alone in the apartment, and, thanks to her thunderous Beagle bark, the entire neighborhood knew it. The neighbors in adjacent apartments were complaining, and tensions were high.

Solution: Upon meeting (and falling in love with) Clare and talking to JoAnne, I found that the only sign of distress Clare showed was barking. No scratching at the door, panting, or accidents. Furthermore, according to neighbors, the barking didn't last all day. Clare would wail when JoAnne left for work, when she heard someone in the hallway, or when there was a loud noise, like a delivery truck, outside. At all other times, she was quiet. This led me to believe that she did not have true separation anxiety and that, with management and time, Clare would become more comfortable alone in the apartment, and her howls would subside. We implemented these changes:

- JoAnne put white noise by the front door and shut the windows. This drowned out the exterior noises that were setting Clare off.
- JoAnne blocked off the foyer, so Clare couldn't sit next to the front door and simply wait for a noise to bark at.
- When JoAnne left for work, she gave Clare a stuffed Kong, which worked wonders. However, after a few days of this, her downstairs neighbor was complaining of banging sounds in the morning, which we realized was Clare playing with her Kong (like a good girl!). To fix this, I showed JoAnne how to take a thin rope, tie a knot at one end, run the rope through the smaller hole of her Kong Classic, and then tether the Kong to a table leg in a carpeted area. Clare could then push the tethered Kong around on only a small area of carpet, which absorbed the shock of the bouncing rubber, and the neighbors subsequently stopped their own howling.
- A dog walker started taking Clare for a walk with another dog in her building, which let Clare blow off some steam midday.
- JoAnne explained the situation to her neighbors, which bought her some extra time in those first few weeks.

After a week, Clare's wails became noticeably less frequent. After about one month, she had settled into her new routine and come to terms with the sounds of city living. The barking was no longer an issue, and now everyone, including her neighbors, can enjoy Clare's beautiful beagle smile without wincing from the voice behind it.

cheer in an encouraging tone when he's nearby. By the fourth repetition, I am completely silent and still—until he finds the treat, and then I can't help but cheer.

From there, you can build up to hiding several treats in a room, placing them while the dog is out of sight. Whenever you use a treat with a new smell (or even a toy), show it to the dog first so he knows what to look for. Finally, once he understands the game, set it up right as you're leaving. You can strategically place his food or treats around a room or just walk through the room, dropping treats as you go. (Just be sure not to let them roll under furniture, unless you want your house redecorated while you're gone.)

If you prefer, you can do a more controlled variation of this game with an old bedsheet or blanket. Sprinkle food or treats on top of and under the blanket and then rustle it up so the treats get nestled in the wrinkles. I use this method for those with a small living space or for dogs who get so excited about the Find It game that they would be jumping on furniture and knocking things over.

Troubleshooting

Problem: My dog gives up before finding the treat(s).

Solution: First, make sure your treats are stinky enough for him to find. Though dogs' sense of smell is incredibly strong, some dogs don't know how to utilize that skill very well. It's also possible that your treat-hiding spots are too difficult for your dog at this moment. Make it easier by making the treats more visible. The whole point is to have fun, so avoid creating a situation that's frustrating rather than rewarding.

Problem: My dog stares at me instead of looking for treats.

Solution: While it's great that your dog looks to you when he needs help, occasionally this behavior can tip into either dependency ("I can't do it! Help me!") or demands ("Hey, human, get it for me. Now!") Neither of these situations is particularly desirable. In most cases, we inadvertently encourage this needy behavior by helping our dogs do things that they are fully capable of doing themselves, so the remedy is simply for you to step back and not get involved. Check your phone, tidy up the room, or relax with a book to tell your dog that this is his game to play, not yours.

Beyond that, there are a few other techniques you can implement if your dog appears clearly confused or distressed. You can make it easier for him to "win" the game, and thus build his independence, by choosing a smaller area, like a bathroom, for him to find treats. Resist the temptation to show him where the treat is, and if he looks at you for help, simply use an encouraging tone, tell him to "Find it," and then break eye contact with him. If your dog gets frustrated and barks at you, that's your cue to walk away. Give him the cold shoulder for about ten seconds; you can even leave the room and shut the door behind you, if possible. This tells the dog, on no uncertain terms, that his barking will yield the opposite of what he wants. Not only will you not help him, but you'll leave the scene altogether.

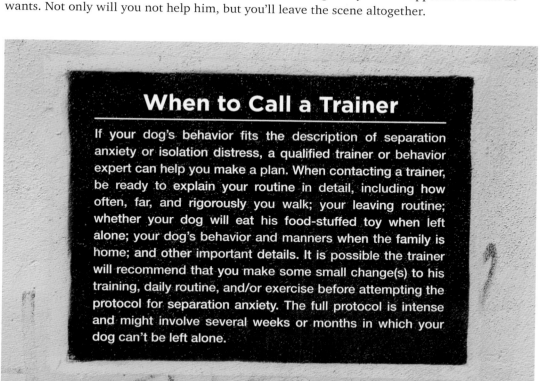

When to Call a Trainer

If your dog's behavior fits the description of separation anxiety or isolation distress, a qualified trainer or behavior expert can help you make a plan. When contacting a trainer, be ready to explain your routine in detail, including how often, far, and rigorously you walk; your leaving routine; whether your dog will eat his food-stuffed toy when left alone; your dog's behavior and manners when the family is home; and other important details. It is possible the trainer will recommend that you make some small change(s) to his training, daily routine, and/or exercise before attempting the protocol for separation anxiety. The full protocol is intense and might involve several weeks or months in which your dog can't be left alone.

MORE USEFUL TRAINING FOR URBAN DOGS

When I initially meet private training clients in their homes, they often say, "I want my dog to be well mannered. What should I teach him?" My answer is always, "Well, it depends. What kind of unwanted behaviors or habits would you like to change?" I've never taught two dogs exactly the same things in the same way because every dog's personality and every family's needs are unique. In the sidebars profiling my clients' dogs throughout the book, you can see how each owner overcame certain behavior problems using a combination of management and training techniques. Perhaps one of their stories will correlate to an issue you're having with your own dog. Even in my own home, I've taught different behaviors to each of my dogs, based on their needs. The two current dogs in my home are as different as night and day. I spent a great deal of effort teaching Leave It and Walk with Attention to Batman, our little dictator who has always had his own agenda. We still practice these behaviors once a day. Given Batman's naturally bossy personality, he has to sit for everything: his meals, permission to join me on the couch, and so on.

Beans, on the other hand, automatically lies down whenever she wants something; I don't even have to ask. I didn't bother to teach her to sit for two years because she already had such a solid Down, which, frankly, accomplishes the same goal as sitting. On walks, she is cautious and in tune to what I'm doing. For instance, if she picks up street garbage, all I have to do is gasp (my natural reaction), and she instantly spits it out. With her, however, I feared she would wiggle out of her harness and be gone in a flash if she were startled or if her prey drive kicked in when a squirrel crossed our path. Therefore, we practiced Emergency Recall until the cows came home—or the Beans came home, in this case. We also counterconditioned extensively to squirrels, cats, dogs, and other moving targets. So you can pick and choose what kind of training your dog needs.

The behaviors in this chapter can help you get that polite urban dog who is the envy of your friends and neighbors. A dog who can heel through intersections, lie quietly next to you at the outdoor café, and come when called is a dog you can take anywhere. Teaching your dog general good manners can actually enrich his life immensely, as polite dogs will be welcome at family events, able to travel with you, and invited to playdates. Rude dogs, on the other hand, have to stay home. The behaviors that follow should be practiced outside, when you're on walks or hanging out in the park, so they become part of your regular routine.

Note: If you are confused by any of the terminology in this chapter, reread Chapter 1.

SIT
How to Teach Sit

1. Place a treat in one hand, palm facing up. This will become a lure. Start with your hand barely an inch above your dog's nose and guide his nose slightly up and backward, which will cause him to lean back and lower his rear end. Move your hand very slowly so your dog's nose can easily follow the lure. The gesture looks like you are scooping something up with your hand in slow motion, right above the dog's nose.

2. Your dog will rock back to follow the treat, ultimately sitting. Mark with "Yes!" at the moment his rear hits the floor, and then reward. If he stands or jumps up while you're giving him the reward, snatch the reward away and start over. He must be sitting while he gets his treat. Get four-for-four.

◀ To teach a Sit, put a treat in your palm and lure the dog into the sitting position. Rachel places her hand just above Malik Jr.'s nose.

◣ She then moves her hand, palm up, slightly behind Malik Jr. and up, causing him to rock back into a Sit. This is the moment to mark "Yes!"

▼ He only gets the treat if he remains in a sitting position.

3. Add the verbal cue "Sit" before you lure with a treat. Get four-for-four. Remember to say the cue only once, and then make it happen by luring.

4. Now remove the treat from your luring hand. It is now a cue, not a lure. You will say "Sit" once and guide your dog with an empty hand. Reward from your other hand, which was hidden behind your back, or from your pocket. Get four-for-four.

5. Gradually make your cue less and less dramatic. Each time, elevate your body position a few inches so your hand is no longer right in front of the dog's nose.

From there, practice Sit in many places, both indoors and outdoors. When you start to practice in a new context (a new location or in the presence of a new kind of distraction), you will probably need to start from Step 1 and build back up. Once your dog is a pro at sitting in various locations, you can start to wean him off the treats. Do this by asking for a Sit and, when he sits, mark and cheer but don't reward with food. Encourage him to get up, and ask for a second Sit.

This time, mark and reward. Moving forward, ask your dog for a few Sits in a row, treating randomly. This will get your dog comfortable with not always getting a food reward. That being said, if your dog performs a Sit in a difficult scenario (for example, in the presence of another dog or a fun toy), it is only fair to reward him for his hard work.

Troubleshooting

Problem: My dog bends his head back but won't sit.

Solution: First, rule out a medical reason for his reluctance to sit, such as soreness or arthritis. Also, make sure the problem isn't due to handler error by recording your training session or watching yourself in a mirror. It will be much easier to see from this perspective if you're luring too fast, which causes the dog to lose the lure, or luring too high, which causes him to jump up. Assuming your lure is spot-on, it's possible that your dog is too excited or distracted to follow the lure into a full Sit. In this case, you can "shape" the behavior, meaning you will reward the dog for any small increment towards sitting. First, mark and reward your dog as he tilts his head up as you lure. Get four-for-four. Then, mark and reward only when he tilts farther back and get four-four-four. Eventually, his whole body will rock back; mark and reward and get four-for-four. Ultimately, he will rock all the way back into a Sit. Jackpot! Reward that full Sit with several treats, one after the other, and celebrate.

Problem: My dog will sit but then pops up immediately.

Solution: Only sitting dogs get the treat. Let go of the treat slowly, so if your dog pops up into a Stand as he gets the treat, you can snatch it away. He just lost his reward. This is a great opportunity for a dog to problem-solve: if he wants the treat, what should he do to get it? If your pup corrects himself by immediately sitting down again, he can have the treat. Good choice! If your dog does not correct himself and continues to stand or jumps up, give an NRM of "Oops" to indicate he's done the wrong thing, wait a few moments, and try again.

Problem: When I say "Sit," my dog sits for a moment and then lies down.

Solution: The solution has two considerations. First of all, make sure that if you are also teaching your dog to lie down, you do not train in this sequence: "Cassie, sit. Cassie, down. Good girl! Here's your treat." This teaches Cassie that every Sit is followed by a Down, which is followed by a treat. Cassie, being clever, will hear your cue "Sit" and assume that the next cue will be "Down," so she'll skip the middleman and go right to the Down, even if you've only asked for a Sit. You can easily prevent this by silently (without a verbal "Sit" cue or visual cue) waiting for your dog to sit before asking for a Down. Most dogs, when they know it's training time, will automatically sit without the need for a verbal or visual cue. This allows you to start the Down from a sitting position but does not negatively impact your Sit cue.

Second, you can help your dog learn to sit, but not lie down, by accelerating your marking and rewarding of Sit. Once Cassie sits, immediately mark, reward, and release with "OK"—don't wait for her to slump into a Down. Practice several repetitions at this faster pace. Once Cassie is consistently sitting and not lying down, start the next activity: "Sit" Actually Means "Stay."

"SIT" ACTUALLY MEANS "STAY"

When we teach our dogs to sit, we're really asking them to sit and then stay there for at least a few moments. This version of Sit will reward the dog not just for putting his rear on the ground, but for keeping it there. Finally, we will add a release word so he knows when it's OK to get up. This teaches your dog impulse control because remaining in a calm sitting position will get him far more rewards than if he were to sit momentarily and jump back up. With practice, he'll be able to sit for longer and longer, which means he will be calm for longer and longer, too. Additionally, this behavior also teaches your dog to remain in the desired position (sitting) even if you have to turn away from him.

While your dog is in the Sit position, you will look away from him briefly. This will teach him to follow your cue even when you break eye contact with him. In real life, you might have to ask him to sit while you turn or walk away, which takes a lot of impulse control on the dog's part, so you need to teach him how to sit for an extended period of time without relying on your eye contact.

How to Teach "Sit" Actually Means "Stay"

1. Ask for a Sit. Your dog sits. Pause one second and look away from your dog; then mark "Yes!" and reward while he's still in the Sit. (Depending on the dog, you may be able to pause for several seconds. Work at your dog's level and don't make it too hard.)
2. After rewarding, say "OK" to release the dog. You may need to pat your leg so your dog gets up. The release word basically means, "All finished; no more rewards."
3. After each successive Sit, add another one- or two-second pause before you mark and reward. So if your dog's first repetition was Sit, one-second pause, mark, reward, release, then his next rep will be Sit, three-second pause, mark, reward, release. Remember to look away or turn away during the pause. Work methodically and don't "test" your dog. If you attempt this exercise in a new environment, start from Step 1 and work your way up.

Troubleshooting

Problem: My dog breaks the Sit early. He stands up before I can mark and reward.

Solution: Lower your criteria; it sounds like you are pushing him beyond his capabilities. If your dog breaks the Sit, mark with an NRM of "Oops" or "Uh-uh." This marks the moment of his mistake and tells him he won't be getting his reward. Bummer! Then, evaluate the environment and ask yourself why it didn't work this time. Did you jump ahead from four seconds to ten seconds? Did you move to a new spot? Did you step farther away from the dog? Is he too excited from just playing fetch? Adjust accordingly and go back to the previous step (say, four seconds, if that's where he was successful). Get four-for-four before proceeding, which will ensure that your dog really knows what you're asking and isn't just guessing.

When training, be aware of your body language. This handler's feet should be facing the same direction as the dog during Side Sit.

SIDE SIT/STAY AT STREET CORNERS

The next time your dog is near you, ask him to sit and watch what he does. Did he walk over in front of you, face you, and then plop his bum on the ground? Of course he did, because that's how we usually teach Sit. He would never even think to sit from any other angle. The benefit of the Side Sit is that the dog is next to you and facing the same direction as you, which is useful when waiting at crosswalks or for an elevator or in any other situation in which you'll be moving forward momentarily. Once your dog has learned that Sit actually means Stay and is able to keep his rear on the ground for at least a few seconds, you can transfer this to a Side Sit. It's not important to me if it's the right or left side, but if you train a Side Sit on both sides, first train one side fully and then the other side to avoid confusion.

How to Teach Side Sit

1. Have a treat in the hand closest to your dog. Walk a few steps with your dog on a short leash so that he's close to you. If your dog is still learning how to walk politely, it's OK to simultaneously walk and lure him with the treat at nose level to keep him next to you.
2. Come to a halt and use the treat to lure your dog into a sitting position, just like the previous Sit exercise, except now your hand is next to you, not in front of you. Don't say "Sit" yet.
3. Once his rear is on the ground at your side, you can give more than one treat to encourage him to stay in that position for several seconds. Once he swallows the last treat, release him from sitting with "OK" and start to walk. Get four-for-four.
4. You'll do the same sequence as before, but add the verbal cue "Sit" before luring him into the position. The sequence will be Sit cue, lure into Sit position, mark, reward, release. Get four-for-four.

The idea of Heel is for the dog to walk at your side, neither pulling ahead nor lagging behind.

If Heel is proving problematic for you in general, you'll benefit from using the techniques in Chapter 5 first. I find that dogs who have already learned to Walk with Attention and understand the New Yorker walk are receptive to learning to heel because they have already practiced underlying concepts that contribute to polite leash walking.

PLACE AT THE OUTDOOR CAFÉ

We New Yorkers love our dogs. We also love our morning brunches and evening cocktails, particularly at outdoor cafés in the summer. Nothing can beat combining our loves by taking our dogs out for a meal or drink with us on a mild summer day. This simple variation of Place with Duration from Chapter 3 teaches your dog to lie on a mat or towel while you enjoy your drink.

How to Teach Place at the Outdoor Café

1. Bring your dog's mat, water bowl, and either a long-lasting chewy or many small treats.
2. Lay the mat next to or under your chair, and cue "Place" as in Chapter 3.
3. When your dog settles on the mat, give him the chewy, and your job is done. If you prefer the treats, give him one treat as often as is needed to keep him settled on the mat.
4. Keep in mind that he might need some breaks, either to stretch or go potty. Be attentive to his needs; it's unrealistic to expect an excitable dog to stay in one spot for an extended period of time.

DOWN

Down has several applications. For our purposes, it is most important as a component of Place, particularly when your dog will be on his mat for extended periods, such as while you're eating dinner. Down is also useful as a starting point to teach certain tricks, such as Play Dead or Roll Over. Finally, because Down is a naturally relaxing position, it can have a calming effect on excitable or nervous dogs.

How to Teach Down

1. Lure your dog into a sitting position or wait for your dog to sit on his own. (Avoid saying the cue "Sit." If you teach your dog the sequence of Sit and then Down, you run the risk of having a dog who gets so used to the Sit-Down pattern that he automatically goes into a Down even if you've only asked for a Sit.) No reward yet.
2. Position your hand so it looks like a hand puppet, with a treat pinched between your thumb and other fingers. This will be your lure. Draw an imaginary "L" shape, starting with a straight line from the dog's nose down to the floor, from "nose to toes." Pause here. Some dogs will slouch into a Down as they try to nibble the treat. If your dog isn't lying down yet, drag the lure out horizontally, away from dog's body and toward you. Drag the lure slowly, so the dog's nose can easily follow your hand.
3. Once his rear end and front elbows are on the ground, mark and reward on the floor between his front paws. This will keep him in the Down position while eating the treat. Once he has finished his treat, you can release with "OK." Get four-for-four.
4. Next, add the verbal cue "Down" right before you lure. Get four-for-four.
5. Remove the treat from your hand. Now, your hand is a cue, not a lure. Reward from your other hand, which was hidden behind your back, or from a pocket. Get four-for-four.
6. Now you can start elevating your signal hand and your body so you don't have to reach all the way to the floor. With each repetition, stop your hand 1–2 inches short of the previous rep.
   - If your dog gets confused at any point, go to the previous step (reaching your hand a little lower) and get four-for-four.

Troubleshooting

Problem: My dog doesn't want to lie down.

Solution: There are a few things you can tweak to make it easier for your dog to lie down.

- First, make sure it's not due to discomfort. When you practice, start on a soft surface, like a rug or blanket. Some dogs are not comfortable lying on a hard floor. On the flip side, if you started on a carpet and had no luck, switch to a hard surface. In some cases, when you lure a dog down on a wood or tile floor, his front legs spread out as his nose follows the treat down; thanks to a little gravity, you've got a Down!
- Some dogs don't respond to the L-shaped lure, so you can get creative. Try luring straight down from nose to toes without dragging it the lure toward you. Hold the treat between the dog's toes for several seconds because he might choose to dip into a Down to eat the treat. Once his front elbows and rear are on the floor, you can release the treat from your hand. If this doesn't work, use the L-shaped lure, but reverse the direction,

◄ I start by slowly luring from Susu's nose to her toes, straight down to the floor between her paws.

◄ Susu bends down to follow the treat. Some dogs will lie all the way down at this stage.

◄ I slowly pull the treat toward me. As Susu leans forward to follow it, her elbows drop into a Down. This is the moment to mark and reward, while she's still in the Down position.

so once your treat is on the floor, push it just an inch or two toward the dog. Some dogs will rock backward into a Down when lured this way.

- If your dog won't bring his elbows all the way down, or he pops up halfway through the lure, you'll need to "shape" the Down. This means you'll reward him for baby steps toward a full Down. The first time, lure a little bit down and mark and reward him for just stretching his neck lower. Get four-for-four neck stretches. Next, tighten the criteria and lure a few inches lower and reward for a more dramatic stretch. With repetition and a little patience, your dog will start to drop one or both shoulders as he reaches down. Great! That's a new milestone, so now you'll only reward for stretches with a slightly dropped shoulder. Keep rewarding for partial progress until you get a full Down. It might not happen in one training session, but the slow-and-steady approach will ultimately lead to a dog who happily lies down on cue.

Problem: My dog will only lie down if I bring my hand cue all the way to the floor.

Solution: When you are ready to start elevating your hand (meaning that you have fully practiced Steps 1–5 of Down), make sure to elevate your hand only about an inch higher than the previous repetition. This means that on your first rep, your hand will stop its downward motion about an inch from the floor. Once your hand reaches that point, hold it there for at least five seconds to give your dog ample time to think about how to respond. He might be confused. If your dog shows hesitation at any point, it would be a good idea to get four-for-four at that level before elevating your hand any higher. If your dog does not respond to your cue at all, then go to an easier level (with your hand cue a little closer to the ground) and get four-for-four before advancing.

Problem: My dog starts to lie down but then pops up when I give him the treat.

Solution: Use your NRM of "Oops" or "Uh-uh" to identify at exactly what point your dog lost his chance for the treat. For example, if your dog puts his front elbows and rear end on the ground but then pops up, mark that exact moment with your NRM and take your reward away. If your dog lies down and starts to nibble the treat but stands up while eating, snatch (what's left of) the treat away and use your NRM. He'll learn that he only gets the treat if he remains in the Down position.

DROP IT

We discussed Leave It in Chapter 5 as a way to prevent your dog from grabbing garbage or other (in)edibles. But what if he already has something forbidden in his mouth? That's where Drop It comes in handy. The concept of spitting something delicious out doesn't exactly come naturally to every dog. After all, he picked it up for a reason, didn't he? By following these steps, you can teach your dog to enjoy Drop It by making a positive association with dropping a street goodie. I recommend training Drop It in very short sessions, just two or three reps, and then end on a good note with a super-tasty treat. We want it to be fun, not frustrating.

As there are four levels of teaching Drop It, and it takes time and practice before you're ready to use this cue on walks. Think of Level 1 as an elementary-school Drop It, Level 2 as a middle-school Drop It, and so on. Asking your pup to drop an actual chicken bone on the

dogs, it can be stressful and lead to confrontation.) Bring your highest value treats. Walk your dog around the park and occasionally ask for a Hand Target. Vary the situation so that you ask for a Touch sometimes when there is no major distraction and other times when a squirrel is crossing your path or a dog is barking nearby. Practice until your dog is reliably hand targeting.

3. Now you need an intermediate step between on- and off-leash. I recommend getting a long line (not a retractable leash) of 20 feet or more and going to the park with your dog and lots of high-value treats. As you walk around, give your dog the feeling that he's free by letting out the long line. Occasionally, as you're walking in a relatively quiet area, do a Touch Recall; when he comes to you, reward him and then send him back out to explore more. What he will learn is, *Wow, when I came to my human, not only did I get a hot dog, but I got to go back to sniffing. Recall is the best!* Repeat this occasionally.

4. Once he can return to you on the long line, start practicing in the presence of distractions, still on the long line. You're asking a lot of him now because there are both distractions present and a longer distance between you two, so reward handsomely with a jackpot the first time your dog responds to your "Touch" cue.

5. Finally, your dog is ready for the park. As with the previous step, it's important to practice Hand Targeting occasionally throughout the playtime at times when you can easily sneak your dog a treat without his friends noticing. Then, send him back to play.

Troubleshooting

Problem: My dog has learned that when I call him, it means it's time to go back home. Now he ignores me when I cue "Touch."

Solution: This means you need to beef up your practice of Hand Targeting in other scenarios. Dogs are very perceptive, so if the only time you do a Hand Target is at the end of his playtime, he will quickly learn not to come to you because that means the end of the fun. Practice more Hand Targets both on leash and off, with only positive consequences. When off leash, give him his reward and then allow him to go back and play. This makes the Hand Target part of the fun itself rather than a signal that the fun is about to end.

TAKING TRIPS IN A PET CARRIER

It's a common, and often entertaining, sight to see dogs of all shapes and sizes being carried in bags, backpacks, and strollers on the New York City subways. The city's rule essentially permits dogs to ride the subway provided they can fit in a bag. This has led to hilarious interpretations, including large-breed dogs stuffed into hiking backpacks, and even one hefty Pit Bull mix being "carried" in a giant blue IKEA bag with holes cut out for his legs; the dog, wrapped in the bag, walked himself onto the subway. (If you ever need a good laugh, do an online search for "NYC dogs in bags.") Regardless of your dog's size, I recommend a ventilated carrier that zips fully closed to ensure that your dog is securely in the bag. It's not just a matter of your dog's becoming scared or excited and jumping out. First of all, not all passengers appreciate your dog's furry face practically on their laps. There is also the possibility of the bag flipping over, getting caught on an object, or experiencing some other accident that could cause your dog to fall out. As cute as the tote-style carriers are, if your dog simply shifts his weight too heavily where the head opening is, he could spill out. These open bags may technically be against the rules on public transportation in your city anyway.

Before getting on that train, your dog needs to learn how to get into his carrier. Depending on your dog's build and the bag's structure, you might have to lift your dog into the bag, but, if possible, I prefer to let the dog step into the bag on his own.

The following steps are just a guide. Some dogs will leap right into the bag with an "All right, let's go!" enthusiasm, while others could be suspicious of this new contraption for a while. Work at your dog's pace, and if you have to add more intermediate steps than are listed here, that's fine.

How to Get Your Dog into the Carrier

1. First, get your dog interested in the bag. Put a few treats (or toys, if your dog prefers) in the bag, place the bag on the floor for five minutes, and walk away. You might have to put it on its side so your dog can access the treats more easily. I suggest walking away because this is the time for the dog to build a "relationship" with the bag without your unintentional interference. Repeat this activity several times until your dog is eagerly, and without hesitation, diving his head in for the snacks.

2. Now you can start to get him into the carrier. If the bag's shape and size permits, you can lure him with a treat into the carrier and then give him several treats while he's inside.

   - He might be hesitant to put his whole body in the carrier. In this case, you can reward him several times for just putting one front paw in. When he finally chooses to put the second front paw in the carrier, give him a huge "jackpot" reward while both paws are in the carrier. (From this point on, only two paws will get him a reward.) Gradually work your way up to all four paws inside, treating with an extra-big jackpot the first time another paw goes in.

   - If your dog can't get into the bag himself, you can pick him up, place him in the bag, and give a jackpot while he's inside the bag. If he seems uncomfortable, it's fine to start with only a few seconds in the bag—just long enough to eat his treats—and then remove him before he tries to jump out.

3. Once your dog will comfortably go into the bag, you can add a verbal cue.

Choose a word or phrase, for instance, "Get in your bag," and then guide him into the bag as before. Practice several times.

4. Now it's time to start moving the bag with your dog in it. In the beginning, just gently carry (or roll, if the bag has wheels) the carrier around your home, dropping a treat into the carrier every few seconds. If your dog likes his regular dry food, you could give him his meal this way, tossing a few pieces of food in the carrier at a time. You may only get a few steps the first time, which is still good progress. Make sure to release him from the bag before he decides he's had enough. Practice in short intervals until your dog seems to understand the "game" and is comfortable being carried in the bag for several minutes.

5. For your first outing in the carrier, go somewhere your dog will love: the park, the pet-supply store, or a friend's house—not the vet's office! The goal is to show him that the carrier is part of a fun adventure. Bring a high-value chewy and some extremely high-value treats. Give your dog the chewy as soon as he gets in the bag. This will keep him busy during the entire commute, so he is far less likely to notice (and therefore panic about) unusual sounds or movement on the train. When you anticipate your dog will experience a potentially startling event, such as a noisy train pulling into the station, drop a few pieces of your extremely high-value treat into the carrier. This prevents the loud noise from making a negative impact on him.

6. While on the train, keep your dog securely in the bag and decline people's requests to pet your dog. The first few rides are likely to be somewhat stressful for your pup, so he would probably be happier left alone to work on his chewy.

You're likely to find that, after a few rides to the park, your dog has learned that the carrier, and even the noisy train, is a pretty awesome thing. In my household, if Batman and Beans even hear me pulling the carriers out of the closet, it quickly becomes a symphony of excited wails and the clicking of the dogs' nails on the floor as they scamper in circles. If I place the bags on the floor, both dogs leap on top of them and try to dig their way into the still-zipped-up bags. To say they like going out in their carriers would be an understatement.

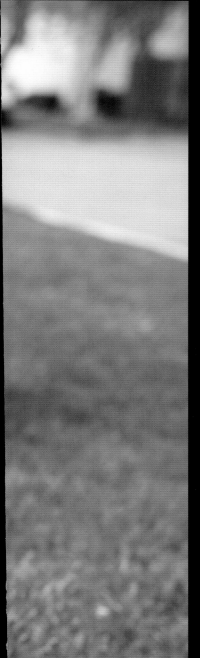

ADDITIONAL CONSIDERATIONS FOR URBAN DOG OWNERS

The urban landscape provides numerous activities and opportunities for dogs and their owners. Many of the dogs I know have a social schedule that puts most humans' to shame. A typical Saturday starts with an early romp in the park during off-leash hours. From there, a dog and his humans head to one of the ubiquitous dog-friendly coffee shops to relax until the next stop: the pet-supply stores and doggie boutiques. After a little nap and wardrobe change, it's off to the puppy play group to make some new friends. There's no shortage of special events for urban dogs, either: doggie fashion shows, numerous fundraising events for animal rescues, and the pinnacle of New York high society: the wildly popular Halloween dog parade.

For outgoing and confident dogs, the city provides all the exercise and stimulation they need. However, urban owners are faced with a great amount of responsibility to ensure that they are keeping their dogs safe at all times. Owners of even the most well-behaved city dogs have numerous considerations on a daily basis: whether to tie the dog to a post while they run into the grocery store, the pros and cons of dog parks, how to take public transportation with a dog, indoor versus outdoor potty places, and more. This section aims to address some of the most common nontraining questions I'm asked.

Should I teach my small dog to go potty outside? Inside on a pad? Both?

In the past, I was a firm believer that dogs, regardless of size, should go potty outside. Because, well, they're dogs, and dogs naturally eliminate outdoors. Then I moved to the fifth floor of an

A four-legged participant in New York City's Halloween parade.

aging brownstone with funhouse-inspired stairs. Shortly after, we took in a grouchy hospice dog named Owen who had to be carried up and down those stairs four times a day, rain or shine, as he snapped like a crocodile all the way. (In his defense, I'm sure Owen was in pain while we carried him.) Suddenly, pee pads didn't seem like such a terrible idea! So now my answer to the question, "Should I use pads indoors?" is "Weigh your options."

Pads have some merit. Having an ever-present potty spot can give you and your pup peace of mind if you get caught in traffic and your dog ends up home alone for a long period of time. While a pad should never be an excuse for not walking a dog, it gives you a solid backup plan on days when either you or your dog walker is too sick to get out of bed. Elderly

Indoor potty pads can come in handy for urban dog owners.

dogs or dogs on certain medications can also benefit from the convenience of pads. I imagine it must be very stressful for a dog who really needs to go potty but doesn't have access to the outdoors. A pad easily solves this problem (provided your dog is taught to use it). Moreover, there are weather considerations. If your dog balks at rain, wind, or snow, he might be so intent on hurrying home that he doesn't fully empty his bladder or bowels while outside. If you live in a place like New York that heavily salts the streets and sidewalks after a mere dusting of snow, it might be nice to have the pee pads so you don't have to walk your dog on salty sidewalks, which can irritate his paws.

On the flip side, consider the drawbacks of pee pads before deciding to pad-train your dog. If your dog is trained to go potty on a pad, you should commit to having the pads out all the time, not just when the weather is inclement. Inconsistent rules lead to accidents. This means that you will have a pad as part of your home decor for the rest of your dog's life. It also means that wherever your dog travels, a pad goes, too. (I actually see this as a positive. Imagine you are on a train or in an airport and your dog has to go potty. You can whisk him to the restroom, lay down a pad, and your dog will be able to relieve himself.) There is another potential downside of having pads on your floor: it's possible that your dog will prefer using the pads over going outside. Let's face it, a pad is a more convenient and less distracting place to go potty than the noisy, crowded city streets. Some dogs forget that outside is also a viable place to potty, and they simply stop eliminating outside altogether. You should still walk your dog regularly, of course, but he may end up holding it until he gets back home to the pad.

One notable problem with pee pads is that, occasionally, dogs who poop on their pads when no one is home—you know where I'm going with this, right?—eat their poop. It's gross but relatively common, and if you're not there to intervene by immediately cleaning up the poop,

Whether training your pup to pads or to outdoors, watch for signs that he has to "go."

you have no defense against it. The proper name for this unsavory habit is coprophagia, and you can purchase products that, when given orally, curb such snacking tendencies by making stool taste bad (as if it weren't bad enough already). Generally, these products get mixed reviews from consumers, so the most effective solution is simply to not let your dog go potty in the house.

Before you choose whether or not to keep pee pads in your home, make a list of pros and cons. This is a decision you only want to make once, because going back and forth between pads and no pads will confuse your dog, and confusion leads to accidents. But let's say you have been using pads and have had enough; starting tomorrow, you want your dog to eliminate outside only. I recommend going cold turkey rather than slowly phasing the pads out. Just rip the bandage off, so to speak. Follow these steps to teach your dog that the pads no longer exist, and outside is the only potty option. Note that these steps are for dogs roughly six months and older. Younger puppies will require more supervision and more frequent outings to relieve themselves.

- Choose a day when you don't have any plans. If you have a typical weekday schedule, start on a Saturday morning and don't make any important plans for the weekend. You might be spending a lot of time on housetraining in the beginning, but if you stick to the program strictly for the first few days, it will be a much smoother road after that.
- The moment you wake up, remove the pad(s), never to be seen again. For added measure, I like to block the area where the pad was to prevent your dog from going potty in his "usual" spot after you've removed the pad. If you had a pad in a bathroom, keep the door closed; if it you had a pad in an open area, use an exercise pen to block the area or move some large furniture to cover the spot. Old habits die hard, so blocking his access to the old potty spot(s) will facilitate your training.
- As soon as you remove the pad(s), don't delay. Whisk the little guy outside to a grassy (if possible) potty spot and bring really tasty treats. Give him a few minutes to do his business. If he goes potty outside, celebrate with cheers and treats at the moment he's finished doing his business. If he doesn't go potty after several minutes, bring him back in the house. Once inside, it's essential to confine him so he won't sneak off and go potty on the floor. If your dog is comfortable in a crate, his crate is the best place to prevent him from having accidents during housetraining. If he doesn't have a crate or doesn't like his crate, you can tie his leash to your waist or hold him in your arms so that he can't quietly sneak into another room and go potty without your knowledge.

- Five minutes later, back outside you both go. Give him a few minutes to go potty outside. If he potties, hooray! Treat time! If he doesn't, head back inside for five more minutes of crating or holding.
- Repeat this sequence until he finally goes potty outside. Eventually he will have to eliminate, and, once he does, you reward him with cheers and treats.
- Go back inside. If you are absolutely certain that he's empty, it's safe to let him eat his breakfast and have free access to the house as usual. However, if you have any suspicion that he might have an accident, you need to either confine him safely (such as in a crate) or keep him under your direct and constant supervision. Don't allow him to sneak off out of your sight, even for a second.
- Repeat this every few hours throughout the day; every time you think he's ready to go potty, whisk him outside. If he does not eliminate outside, keep him safely confined or keep your eyes on him and then bring him back out again. If he's allowed to go into another room unsupervised, you may find yourself cleaning up pee very shortly after.
- Your dog might have an accident in the house. While unpleasant, this is part of the process and a useful learning experience. Because you have either confined him or are watching him constantly, you will be able to catch him in the act. Interrupt him with a clap (but avoid yelling; he's already stressed enough by this new routine) and immediately take him outside to finish his business in the appropriate place. If he does, then he gets the same cheers and treats as always. If he doesn't do anything outside, then simply make a mental note of the circumstances surrounding the accident: what time it was, how long it had been since his last meal or drink, if he was excited, active, whining, etc. This information can help you prevent a future accident by knowing his "gotta go" signs.
- If you find that he snuck off and had an accident when you weren't looking, do not punish him. He didn't make the mistake, you did. Prevent situations like this from happening again by either confining him or watching him more carefully.
- Starting on Monday, give yourself extra time to take your dog outside (maybe more than once) in the morning before you leave the house. It's likely your dog will need to be confined while you're at home until you are sure he is fully housetrained.

Housetraining means being consistent, no matter the weather.

Some dogs pick up on housetraining very quickly, while others take months before I consider them reliably housetrained. With this kind of training, err on the side of caution. If you have any doubt at all about your dog's ability to hold it while you're gone, confine him. The biggest mistake many owners make is assuming their dog is housetrained when he is not, so they give him free access to the house while they're out, and if he has an accident, no one is there to address it. That's how bad habits start. When in doubt, confine your dog to his crate or gate him in a small room, like a bathroom, so he cannot soil your carpets or floors while you're gone.

Enlist the help of a dog walker for midday walks and potty breaks, using the guidelines in Chapter 6. I recommend having a very strict routine—in which your dog is always in your sight or confined while you're home and always safely confined when you're not home—for at least one month. After one month with zero accidents, start to give him a little more freedom. You can leave him home alone in one room for short periods while you pick up the mail or do another quick errand. Check for accidents when you get back; if he has soiled in the room, start the process again until he has had one full month with zero accidents. After each accident-free month, he can have a little more freedom, with access to more rooms and longer durations in the house by himself. With this method, it can easily take six months to give your dog full freedom of the house, but, in my opinion, six months of strict supervision is a much better deal than up to sixteen years of occasional accidents.

Is it OK to tie my dog outside the coffee shop while I run inside?

Short answer: no. Long answer: most definitely not! But why am I so hostile to this seemingly innocuous, time-saving act? There are several reasons, all related to safety. First, consider what the dog is feeling while he's tied to a post on a public street, watching his owner disappear into the blackness of a coffee shop or deli. How stressful that must be for the poor dog, losing sight of his trusted human and being trapped like a sitting duck for any person or other dog who walks past. Passersby, not knowing the dangers of touching a stressed dog, might reach out to pet him, hug him, or put their faces close to his, and he is stuck there, unable to escape. In situations like this, an overwhelmed dog's "fight or flight" instinct could kick in. If he is tied to a pole, he can't perform flight, so his only option is fight. I can't blame a stressed dog who growls, lunges, or snaps at strangers who try to engage with him. Wouldn't you do the same? However, when humans put a dog into a stressful situation, and then the dog lashes out in response, it's almost always the dog who gets blamed.

Additionally, even if your dog is entirely trustworthy while tied and left on the sidewalk, you have no control over what happens while you're not with him. What if a friendly stranger gives him candy containing toxic xylitol? Or perhaps a little girl tries to pet him and, when your dog flinches, the child screams, claiming she's been bitten. (I've seen this happen.) If you're not there to see it or intervene, you have no argument against the enraged, albeit mistaken, parents. Legal accusations of bites rarely end up going well for the dog. Finally, dogs can and do get stolen, either to be kept by the dognapper, sold online, or used as bait for dogfighting rings. As much as you'd love to save fifteen minutes by taking the dog on your coffee run, is that coffee really worth losing your dog forever?

Your city may offer safe alternatives to tying your dog to a pole, such as the high-tech doghouses that have been popping up around New York City. For a fee, you can securely leave

For many reasons, tying your dog outside on the street is never a good idea.

your dog in temperature-controlled doghouses that are strategically placed outside of coffee shops and other establishments. Or you can go the old-fashioned route and simply bring a friend who can wait with your dog while you run inside the shop.

I walk my dog on the same route every day. Is that OK?

I generally recommend you walk your dog in as many directions as possible. Dogs are creatures of habit, and, at first glance, it may seem convenient when they choose a regular morning pee spot. And there is added comfort in knowing your route by heart, even when you're half asleep. However, what happens when your dog's nemesis is hanging out by the morning pee spot and you can't go that way? Or when your usual route is blocked by construction? Suddenly, you have to change your routine, and your dog is thrown off. He refuses to pee, and you get frustrated. You can easily prevent this kind of morning meltdown by taking a different direction each morning or rotating among three or four directions. This will make your dog flexible enough to tolerate unforeseen changes around your neighborhood. It also makes your dog able to handle bigger disruptions, like staying at a friend's house.

Another fantastic way to keep your dog interested in walks is to occasionally let him choose the route. Being a follower can be dull, so give your pup the opportunity to take the reins from time to time. When you allow your dog to take the lead and choose the path, it builds independence and can be very satisfying for the dog. I do this individually with each of my dogs once a week. (Because two dogs will inevitably make two different choices, I need to walk them separately for this activity.) As long as he is safe—meaning no walking in the street, no eating garbage, and no venturing into questionable neighborhoods—you just follow. It's likely your dog will be confused at first, stopping at a crosswalk and looking at you as if to ask, "Which way?" You can simply say, "You pick" and then look away. Eventually, he'll choose a direction, and off you go! Anytime your dog looks to you for instruction, just repeat, "You pick" and wait for him to choose a direction. Once the dog gets the hang of it, you'll see how excited he gets when he can decide where to go. He might even start running; if your body can handle it, run along with him.

I've found this to be a great activity for all kinds of dogs. In my household, Batman is the confident dog, and he seems to find the self-directed walk satisfying and even relaxing because he can set the pace and have near-complete autonomy over the walk. If he wants to sniff a shrub for a full five minutes, I'm not going to stand in his way. Beans, on the other hand, is the nervous one. Letting her lead the walks was awkward at first because she was so used to taking direction from me that she didn't want to choose a direction. But once she caught on to this new style of walking, she was unstoppable. Our walks quickly turned into gallops, and the two of us have explored parts of Brooklyn that I never would have seen otherwise. The once-timid Beans quickly became an adventure junkie during these walks, thinking independently and choosing a new direction each time. Whether bossy or bashful, your dog can also benefit from the occasional self-directed walk.

Should I take my dog to the dog park?

I have mixed feelings about dog parks. For many dogs, it's the highlight of the day and a fantastic way to blow off steam. On the other hand, the unregulated nature of a public dog park means that one bad apple can be frustrating or downright dangerous for all of the other dogs. My preferred off-leash areas are large, open spaces where dogs have several acres to spread out and wander

The dog park should have a designated area for small dogs.

until they find a playmate who matches their size and energy level. Cramped enclosures don't allow dogs to distance themselves from unsuitable playmates. This, in turn, means that your dog might not be able to get away from a bully, which is stressful and potentially unsafe.

If you have a small dog, avoid any dog park that does not have a separate area for small dogs. Large dogs, especially when playing and aroused, can tip into predator mode and perceive a small dog to be prey, with results as horrifying as you would expect. If you feel that there is an unstable dog—regardless of his size—near yours, leave immediately. Inappropriate dog play is not something that owners can resolve, and, contrary to popular belief, the dogs will not work it out themselves (more on that later.) Talking to the owner of the unstable dog will likely make things worse. After all, if the owner were responsible, her dog wouldn't be in the park, terrorizing other dogs, in the first place!

A lot of dog-park conflicts could be prevented if the humans were simply watching their dogs more closely. The best thing you can do is put away your cell phone and stay near enough to your dog that he is aware of your presence. Just showing your dog that you're watching will help keep the play "nice," because dogs are more likely to play politely when they are being actively supervised. Staying near your pup will also give him the ability to retreat to you if he needs assistance. Many people take the attitude of "the dogs will work it out themselves." If all dogs at the park were stable, that might be the case: older dogs would gently correct the young ones for getting too excited, and the younger ones would respect those corrections and tone it down. However, the dog park is a mixed bag, and some of the dogs simply do not belong there, so it's best to be vigilant.

If you watch doggie-daycare attendants overseeing the dogs playing, you will see them constantly intervening to prevent dogs' excitement from escalating into rude or aggressive displays. They do not sit on the sidelines, drinking coffee and letting a bully repeatedly chase or plow over a weaker dog, and neither should you. (Reputable daycare facilities also evaluate every dog's behavior before accepting them, in order to ensure safety.) When at the dog park or play group, don't feel badly about intervening if you think your dog is being bullied or being the bully. By intervening, I mean removing your dog from that situation; I never recommend touching another person's dog. Likewise, if your dog is being chased, and he runs to you for help, assist him by body-blocking (with your body, not your hands) between him and the bully. If your dog is in danger but has run farther away, use your Emergency Recall from

Chapter 5 to call him back. From there, either move to a different part of the park or excuse yourself entirely.

If you're not comfortable with bringing your dog to a dog park, consider supervised play groups, which are offered at many training facilities and doggie daycare centers, usually for a small fee. Many of these groups are divided by size, breed, and/or age. If your dog is of a certain breed, there might be a social group established in your city for enthusiasts of that breed, with regularly scheduled play groups at a facility. These supervised, organized events are my preferred method of dog play because I know that a professional is overseeing the group and will intervene or even excuse dogs who don't play nicely. The owners should still keep an eye on their dogs while playing, but there will always be a knowledgeable human in charge.

Keep in mind that off-leash play is not right for every dog. As discussed in Chapter 6, some dogs would prefer to lounge at home, basking in a sunbeam, rather than romping around with five new doggie friends. While we have great expectations that our dogs should be friendly and easygoing in all social situations, there is nothing "wrong" with a dog who doesn't like to play or doesn't play well with other dogs. It's no different from another highly social species: humans. For instance, I'm perfectly happy getting food delivered and watching a documentary on a Friday night, while other New Yorkers prefer to be part of the action, eating at some hot new restaurant or squeezing themselves up to the front row of a concert. If your dog is more the sunbeam-at-home type than the dog-park type, it's best not to force him to go (just as no one should force me to get out of my sweatpants on a Friday night). Furthermore, if your dog is highly aroused by other dogs, to the point that the play tips into scuffles, replace the dog park with more controlled physical activities. This could mean long runs or, even better, you could try dog sports such as agility, flyball, dog parkour, and others, which are described in more detail later in this chapter.

Lastly, dogs who do not have a solid recall, including Emergency Recall from Chapter 5 and Off-Leash Recall from Chapter 7, are not quite ready for unfenced off-leash environments. Safety always needs to be a higher priority than fun.

What does nice dog play look like?

Entire books have been written on this subject, so this is the short version. Because a picture is worth a thousand words (and a video even more), I recommend watching and rewatching the YouTube series titled "At the Dog Park" by dog expert Sue Sternberg's Great Dog Productions. Similar to children playing cops-and-robbers or wrestling, dog play actually resembles fighting; however, playing dogs give their play partners numerous *metasignals*, which are signals that tell the other dog, "I'm just playing and I don't mean any harm." In brief, these are some signs that indicate nice play:

- The dogs take turns chasing one another or getting on top of one another.
- The dogs' bodies and tails are loose and relaxed (relative to each dog or breed) rather than stiff.
- When the dogs jump up, approach, or play-bite each other, they do it from the side, not directly face-to-face. Approaches from the side are usually not threatening.
- The dogs approach each other with bodies curved.
- They take pauses between play. The pause could be a split second in which the dogs each seem to freeze, and then they resume playing.
- Dogs "play bow" with each other: their forelegs are in a lying-down position and their rear ends are standing up in the air.
- Their mouths are open and their lips relaxed, with commissures (corners) gently pulled back in a sort of smile.

I generally don't worry too much about these things, but will keep an eye on the dog exhibiting the following behaviors:

- Growling or other vocalizations are usually no cause for alarm. However, if your dog's vocalizations continue to get more intense or change in pitch, it could indicate that he's getting overly aroused and needs a break to cool off.

Dogs at play look happy and relaxed.

- *Piloerection*, which refers to the hair on the shoulders and back (hackles) standing up, is another indication of arousal but not necessarily a fight. If the dog's body is generally loose, and he is taking turns with his playmate, there's no need to intervene. If his body has become stiffer, his commissures have moved forward into more of a pucker, or he is not taking turns politely, it's time to give him a break and then find a different playmate.
- Wrestling, chasing, play biting, and pinning another dog down are all part of normal, albeit rather ugly, dog play. As long as the dogs are taking turns, approaching from the sides, and exhibiting the other "play" metasignals I mentioned, there's no need to intervene.
  I intervene when I see these things:
- If one dog is pursuing another but does not stop and switch directions to let the other dog pursue him, it is no longer fun for the chased dog. The same goes for pinning a dog down or biting another dog without a break. While there are a few dogs who like being chased or pinned down and actually invite it, in most cases, the play should be back-and-forth, with the dogs taking turns.
- A dog whose body and/or tail becomes stiff needs to be given a break to cool off. Likewise, remove your dog if his or another dog's vocalizations and/or eyes become increasingly more intense.
- It is rude when one dog is trying to end the play, possibly by walking away, sniffing the ground, or showing teeth, but the other dog is not respecting these signs and continues to pursue. They should be separated.
- When two or more dogs gang up on one dog, I always intervene to prevent bullying.
- When two dogs of very different sizes, ages, play styles, or energy levels interact, I will intervene sooner rather than later, to prevent bullying or injury. In this case, I simply call my dog back to me and move to another area of the park.

How can I channel my active dog's energy in a city?

For some dogs, a walk around the neighborhood or a romp at the dog park just doesn't cut it. Some dogs crave more engagement and stimulation, both mentally and physically. Fortunately, there is a canine sport to fit nearly every dog, and many of these sports are growing rapidly in urban and suburban areas. Canine sports burn calories and build brain power, giving you a tired and satisfied dog at the end of the day. These sports also go a long way to building your communication and bond with your dog because you're learning new tasks together and problem-solving as a team.

As canine sports increase in popularity, it's becoming easier to find training facilities or clubs in your area that offer sport classes, competitions, or both. Even if your local training center doesn't offer classes for the sport of your choice, certain trainers might offer private lessons. Just among the trainers at the Brooklyn Dog Training Center, we teach group or private lessons in agility, rally obedience, flyball, scent games, barn hunt, tricks, musical freestyle, dog parkour, and more. This section will give a brief introduction to some of the most popular—and fun— dog sports. If any of them pique your interest, I recommend watching a variety of videos of the sport online. For instance, by searching for videos of musical freestyle, you're sure to find the best-of-the-best routines from world-class competitions, such as Crufts in the United Kingdom, as well as simpler routines by teams who are just starting out.

Agility to the Rescue

For years, Doggie Academy founder Sarah Westcott, CPDT-KSA, has been competing in agility with her lab mix Hank (or "Hank AX AXJ MXP MJP OF CGC TKA APD RL1," if you count all of his accolades). If you watch Sarah and Hank at an agility trial, they are so in tune to one another that they make it look easy. But it wasn't always that way, as Sarah humorously recalls.

"I started training in agility because I had adopted the worst dog ever. Hank is my now nine-year-old Labrador/Redbone Coonhound mix. Right from the start, he was tough. The first day I brought him home, I put him in a crate and left the room for ten minutes. When I returned, he was staring at me blankly from on top of the ottoman. And he'd peed on the rug.

"I had had dogs before, but none like Hank. If I set him up for success, he failed. If I tried to correct him, I swear he shrugged. Friends recommended I return him to the shelter, and it was an appealing idea. I needed something to occupy this dog—something more than extra walks, trips to the dog park, and food-dispensing toys. I enrolled in an agility class and, despite having to manage Hank's behavior for the entire hour, I enjoyed myself. We started to take classes every week.

"The Brooklyn sidewalks gave Hank and me a surprising number of training opportunities. Everyday objects became agility obstacles: a leftover traffic cone, the stairs on my front stoop, and delivery boxes have all been used in my agility training. As we worked together in agility, we started to become a team. As we became a team, we started to appreciate each other, and Hank started to pay more attention to me. He started choosing me over distractions. This terrible dog and I were bonding!

"Now, Hank is my handsome old man. He's slowed down, but he's still competing in agility, and we've started rally obedience, which is easier on his body. But his best job is as my napping partner. No dog has ever cuddled as hard as Hank. If I had returned him all those years ago, I would have missed out on the amazing dog he is now."

Agility

You've probably caught an agility trial at some point, either on television or in person. If you haven't seen it, you're really missing out! Doggie Academy trainer Amanda Kontakos sums it up: "Agility is a fun, fast canine sport that involves a handler-and-dog team who run together through a course of obstacles, including jumps, tires, tunnels, teeter-totters, dog walks, A-frames, weave poles, and more. In competition, dogs are faulted for dropped jump bars, missed tunnel and weave pole entrances, obstacle refusals, and so on. The dog with the clear course and fastest time wins."

Canine agility equipment at a dog park.

It's an incredible testament to the athleticism of canines, and it exemplifies the ability of humans and dogs to communicate with one another. There are several agility organizations that promote the sport and host trials, such as the United States Dog Agility Association (USDAA). Do a little online digging (for example, on www.usdaa.com), and you'll see that agility organizations have competitive divisions for dogs of all heights and skill levels as well as handlers of all ages.

Agility attracts all types of dogs, from sleek Border Collies to chubby Corgis, and most of the dog-and-handler teams that practice agility with Doggie Academy don't intend to compete—at least not initially. Some are puppies who are just learning to interact with the world; others are energetic dogs who need to channel their excitement; and still others are clever dogs who need to put their minds to work. Agility classes, whether group or private, focus on accuracy and communication between handler and dog. Since the dog is off leash and usually not by the handler's side while running an agility course, he learns to follow the handler's instructions but also to think independently. No one will hoist him onto a teeter-totter or lure him over a jump, so he needs to use his mind to apply the handler's instructions (and quickly!). Because there are usually more than a dozen obstacles in an agility course, and because you can make an infinite number of courses using the

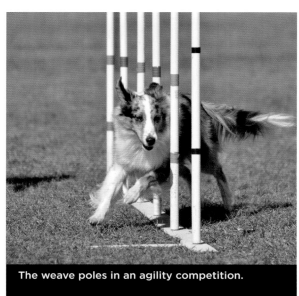

The weave poles in an agility competition.

same obstacles, agility always feels new, fun, and exciting for both dog and handler.

Many cities have dog training facilities that offer agility, at least at the recreational level. At the Brooklyn Dog Training Center, the trainers hold a variety of agility classes: competitive, recreational, small-dog agility, and even puppy agility. While dogs of certain builds and those younger than eighteen months should avoid jumping, they can still benefit from interacting with the other obstacles, including tunnels, weave poles, and teeter-totters, all of which expose them to new challenges in positive, enjoyable ways. Amanda explains, "Agility helps puppies understand that dark tunnels, moving surfaces, and other strange-looking objects aren't actually scary. Entering an agility class at a young age will also teach your dog to focus around the distraction of other dogs and will help him grow into an adult who focuses on you, his human."

Your dog does not have to be perfectly mannered to participate in agility classes. In fact, agility can help some difficult dogs learn better manners and bond more strongly with their owners. See the "Agility to the Rescue" sidebar for a story of how agility saved one owner's sanity and helped her build a relationship with her seemingly unlovable dog.

Keep It Safe

Note that there are safety and age restrictions in certain sports; for instance, dogs younger than eighteen months have to forego the jumps in agility because their bodies are still developing. Likewise, with dog parkour, safety is the main consideration when scoring a dog's performance. Keep your dog's conformation (body type) and safety in mind before attempting any sport.

Rally Obedience (a.k.a. Rally and Rally-O)

Rally is less physically demanding, for both dogs and humans, than agility but still provides a thorough mental workout and some low-impact exercise to boot. A rally course consists of twelve or more sequential tasks that a dog and handler perform together, and the majority is done with the dog in a Heel position to the handler's left. Each task is designated by a sign that lists one or more behaviors, such as "Sit, Down, Sit;" "270-Degree Turn;" "Slow Pace;" or "Weave" (through a set of cones). The dog and handler walk from one sign to the next, performing each required task until they've completed the course. There are a few organizations that hold rally events, including World Cynosport Rally Limited (WCRL). Each organization has different levels of rally, with increasingly difficult tasks at each level. At the higher levels, rally incorporates certain elements of other sports, such as jumping over a jump or retrieving a dumbbell, as in obedience trials.

The beauty of rally is that any dog can do it. Rally is the melting pot of dog sports; at any event, you can find puppies, seniors, active dogs, couch potatoes, blind dogs, and the list goes on. I chose to get started in rally with my Chihuahua mix, Batman, when he was about thirteen years old, and it was perfect for us. Given his age, Batman was not interested in feeling the wind in his fur while speeding through an agility course. With rally, he could physically perform all of the basic required behaviors, and we could tackle the course at our own pace because rally is not a speed event. (There are rules on time limits, but they vary among divisions and organizations.) Essentially, any dog who enjoys training with you is the perfect rally dog. Another great aspect of rally is how easy it is to incorporate into your daily life, even if you don't have a facility or

Amanda and Lucy practicing rally at home.

trainer that offers rally classes. Though an experienced instructor will give you the most targeted advice, there is nothing stopping you from simply printing out free rally signs from WCRL's website (www.rallydogs.com) and, using the tips provided on the same website or using a book for guidance, setting up your own course in your home. It's the perfect rainy-day hobby to engage bored dogs.

Unlike some of the other dog sports, rally teaches a dog to stay close to his handler and wait for explicit instructions from her. This kind of practice can significantly strengthen your dog's general manners on leash as he learns how much fun it is to pay attention to you and work together as a team. When I've either taken or taught group rally classes at the Brooklyn Dog Training Center, the owners often remark how polite their dogs have been since practicing rally. Even if you don't intend to participate in a rally trial, the skills you'll learn in a class can benefit your day-to-day relationship with your dog for years to come.

Rally can help some dogs come out of their shells. Lucy, a young Bichon Frise adopted by trainer Amanda Kontakos, was extremely fearful and overwhelmed in Brooklyn's urban environment, shying away from people and noises. In an effort to boost Lucy's confidence, Amanda and Lucy began participating in canine sport classes simply for recreation, not for competition. Amanda says, "Agility helped Lucy gain confidence on and around different textures, movements, and sounds, while rally obedience helped solidify her overall good manners and responsiveness in a variety of situations and environments. Over time, training in rally gave Lucy something to do and focus on when around stimuli that scared her, and, eventually, we were able to heel past garbage trucks, complete Sit-Stays at busy intersections, and maintain good, calm focus when around strangers. We were even able to participate in a rally obedience trial, where she received a qualifying score. Her progress has exceeded my expectations."

Flyball

Flyball is an adrenaline-pumping canine sport that is open to both mixed and pure breeds. Unlike agility or rally obedience, the 51-foot-long flyball course is the same every time. A flyball heat consists of two four-dog teams who run the course side-by-side as a relay race. Each dog must run over four hurdles, push against a spring-loaded "flyball box," which releases a tennis

ball, and then carry the ball back over the same four hurdles. Once the first dog on the team returns to the starting point, the second dog is released to run. The height of the hurdles is set to accommodate the shortest dog on the team. The first team to have all four dogs complete the course with no errors wins.

However, as with all canine sports, your dog doesn't need to be a speed demon to enjoy flyball recreationally. If you have a dog who loves to fetch and has energy to burn, chances are your dog will naturally take to flyball. If your dog is full of energy but doesn't know how to fetch, don't despair. Fetching a ball is a teachable behavior. Some dogs may not be suitable for flyball, however. Because it's a high-impact, high-speed sport that repetitively puts strain on the same joints and muscles, consider your dog's conformation and your ability to keep him in good physical shape.

Flyball has one benefit that the other sports generally do not: it's a team sport. For the handler, being part of a flyball team provides opportunities for socializing with like-minded individuals and motivating one another to keep improving. Additionally, this sport is an excellent way to teach dogs to focus amid the distractions of other dogs running alongside them and the noises made by the

The dog steps on the box to release the tennis ball.

handlers and other dogs. Flyball also teaches dogs precision because they have to learn the best way to approach the hurdles and negotiate the box to shave off precious seconds from their run. Sometimes it's just hundredths of a second that separate first- and second-place teams.

Musical Freestyle

Musical freestyle lets you and your dog get creative together. Sometimes called "dancing with your dog," freestyle is both a recreational and competitive sport in which you create a routine with your dog, often to the song of your choice. The great thing about freestyle is that, because you make the routine yourself (within certain guidelines), you can choreograph a unique performance that highlights what your dog does best. Routines generally include components of heelwork and tricks; the dog often interacts closely with you (for example, weaving through your legs), but at times he may perform tricks at a distance, too. There are a few organizations that promote the sport and offer competitive titles, but a good starting point is Rally Freestyle Elements (www.rallyfree.com). Depending on the organization, competitors can compete either at live events or by video submission, making freestyle accessible to almost anyone.

Because recreational freestyle requires nothing more than a dog and an imagination, it is a very simple sport to get involved in, and, as such, it's quickly growing in popularity. You may be able to find an instructor, group classes, or even competitions in your area. Freestyle is a fun way to build on your dog's basic skills, such as heeling, targeting, or tricks. Because you don't need any special equipment, you can practice freestyle moves in your home or on the sidewalk, so dogs who aren't comfortable in group classes can still learn routines and compete by video submission, if interested.

Jenn and Terra performing their "Car Wash" freestyle routine.

APPENDIX

SUGGESTED TRAINING PLANS AND CHARTS TO TRACK YOUR PROGRESS

The following section provides sample training plans for the BKLN Manners™ training strategies that require multiple levels of practice. You and your dog might take longer to meet your training goals than the following examples, or you might breeze through them quickly. Either way is fine. The weekly plan for each behavior is simply an example to guide you, and you should adjust your own expectations to fit your dog's situation. There are a few points to keep in mind when tracking your progress:

1. Work at your dog's pace, even if feels slow. Rushing through the levels will ultimately lead to a half-learned Place or an Emergency Recall that works except during real emergencies. Slow and steady practice will actually yield faster progress.
2. When beginning a training session, start with a warm-up that is one or two levels easier than where you finished last time. So if you finished with a thirty-second Place last time, start this session with a fifteen-second Place. This goes for all of the training you do, whether formal training sessions or training that you are integrating into your daily routine (such as teaching a Hand Target while you're out walking your dog).
3. Actually record your results on the chart. It only takes a few seconds, and writing it down will help you prevent confusion and identify problems that may arise. For each box, record the last correct response your dog got. This means that if you finished Place with four-for-four correct at one minute, you'd write "1 min" in that box. This reminds you to start the next session at about forty-five seconds to warm up and then increase the duration in the following reps.

For the first behavior, Check Me Out, you'll see a sample plan that lists goals for days 1, 7, 14, and 21. This doesn't mean your training will take only twenty-one days, but after three weeks of methodical practice, you will have enough of a foundation to be able to continue on your own.

The goal listed for each day is the highest level that the "example" dog achieved. The twenty-one-day plan is followed by a chart. For Check Me Out, I've provided a sample chart to illustrate how to fill in each box to track your dog's progress. On the blank chart, follow this style with your own training, marking the highest level of Check Me Out that your dog achieves each day. The blank charts will take you through the first two weeks of training, but I encourage you to continue keeping track of your progress for as long as needed.

Check Me Out
Sample plan
Day 1 goals:
- Your dog briefly glances at your face in a quiet indoor area.

Day 7 goals:
- Your dog holds three-second eye contact in a quiet indoor area.
- Your dog briefly glances at your face in a quiet outdoor area.
- Your dog briefly glances at your face before you throw his ball, open a door, and the like.

Day 14 goals:
- Your dog holds three-second eye contact in a quiet outdoor area.
- Your dog briefly glances at your face in a mildly distracting outdoor area.
- Your dog holds three-second eye contact before you throw his ball, open a door, and the like.

Day 21 goals:
- Your dog holds five-second eye contact anytime he wants something from you.
- Your dog offers eye contact on walks, occasionally checking in with you.
- Your dog briefly glances at you in a highly distracting outdoor area, such as the park.

A sample chart follows. Your results might look something like this:

	INDOORS FOR TREAT OR "LIFE REWARD"	OUTDOORS FOR TREAT
Day 1	glance for treat	
Day 2	glance for treat, glance for ball	
Day 3	glance for treat, glance for ball	
Day 4	2 sec. for treat, glance for ball	glance in quiet area
Day 5	3 sec. for treat, 1 sec. for ball	glance in quiet area
Day 6	3 sec. for treat, 3 sec. for ball	glance in quiet area
Day 7	3 sec. for treat, 4 sec. for ball	glance in quiet area
Day 8	4 sec. for ball, glance for door	glance in quiet area
Day 9	6 sec. for ball, glance for door	glance in quiet area
Day 10	6 sec. for ball, glance for door	glance in quiet area
Day 11	2 sec. for door	2 sec. in quiet area, glance in mid-noisy area
Day 12	2 sec. for door	2 sec. in quiet area, glance in mid-noisy area
Day 13	5 sec. for ball, 1 sec. for door	3 sec. in quiet area, 2 sec. in mid-noisy area
Day 14	6 sec. for ball, 3 sec. for door	3 sec. in quiet area, 2 sec. in mid-noisy area

Now, track your own progress on the following chart. Don't worry if you backslide a little here and there; however, if you notice that your dog is not making progress over the course of a week, it's time to investigate the cause of the problem. Check the "Troubleshooting" section of the training behavior and, if necessary, contact a trainer using the guidelines in Chapter 1 if you don't know why your dog is struggling.

	INDOORS FOR TREAT OR "LIFE REWARD"	OUTDOORS FOR TREAT
Day 1		
Day 2		
Day 3		
Day 4		
Day 5		
Day 6		
Day 7		
Day 8		
Day 9		
Day 10		
Day 11		
Day 12		
Day 13		
Day 14		

Place, Level 1 (Duration)
Sample plan

Day 1 goals:
- Cue "Place" and lure the dog to his place (as in Steps 1–6) near the front door.

Day 7 goals:
- Empty-hand cue (no lure) to his Place, then reward every 20 seconds for one minute.

Day 14 goals:
- Reward every 30 seconds for three minutes.

Day 21 goals:
- Reward every minute for three minutes.

When you fill out the chart, write down the highest level of Place that your dog reached. For example, on Day 3, you could write, "5 sec. pauses between treat, 30 sec. total." The goal is to systematically extend the pause between rewards, which means that you will also be gradually extending the total time your dog is on his place. Remember that your dog should get four-for-four at that level to be considered a noteworthy achievement. Your training may take more than fourteen days, so I recommend continuing the chart on your own.

Place, Level 2 (Distance)
Sample plan

Day 1 goals:
- Place with you one step away from the mat.

Day 7 goals:
- Place with you 5 feet from the mat.

Day 14 goals:
- Place with you 7 feet from the mat.
- You pause ten seconds before releasing.

Day 21 goals:
- Place with you across the room.
- You pause fifteen seconds before releasing.

You'll notice in the chart that, starting with Week 2, I have added duration into the practice (meaning not only are you standing away from the mat, but you will also pause for longer and longer after your dog goes to his place). If your dog isn't ready to combine duration and distance in Week 2, keep practicing just distance until you are satisfied, and then add duration.

Place, Level 1 (Duration)

	PAUSES BETWEEN TREATS	TOTAL TIME IN PLACE
Day 1		
Day 2		
Day 3		
Day 4		
Day 5		
Day 6		
Day 7		
Day 8		
Day 9		
Day 10		
Day 11		
Day 12		
Day 13		
Day 14		

Place, Level 2 (Distance)

	DISTANCE BETWEEN YOU AND THE MAT	DURATION OF PAUSE BEFORE RELEASING
Day 1		
Day 2		
Day 3		
Day 4		
Day 5		
Day 6		
Day 7		
Day 8		
Day 9		
Day 10		
Day 11		
Day 12		
Day 13		
Day 14		

Place, Level 3 (Distraction)
Sample plan
Day 1 goals:
- The dog stays in his place while you drop an "elementary-school level" item. (See the full Place description in Chapter 3 for the different categories of items.)

Day 7 goals:
- The dog stays in his place while you drop a "high-school level" item.

Day 14 goals:
- The dog stays in his place while you drop a "PhD-level" item.
- The dog stay in his Place while you drop an "elementary-school level" item and simultaneously add distance or duration. (Again, see Chapter 3 for more details on this.)

Day 21:
- The dog is comfortable with varying combinations of duration, distance, and distractions.

Your dog may be ready for a combination of duration, distance, and distraction starting with Week 2, so I have added all three "D" elements to the chart. (If he is not ready by Week 2, that's also fine.) Remember to increase only one "D" at a time.

Place, Level 4 (Doorbell Counterconditioning)
Sample plan
Day 1 goals:
- You play a recording of the doorbell, and your dog goes to his place.

Day 7 goals:
- You cue with a full-volume doorbell, and your dog goes to his place.

Day 14 goals:
- You cue with a full-volume doorbell and invite a calm friend in while the dog is in Place.

Day 21 goals:
- You have a "real" visitor (calm friend) ring and come in while the dog is in his Place.

In the chart, track your progress. Start with increasing the volume of the doorbell ring. Once your dog understand that the full-volume ring means "Place," start adding activity, such as walking to the door, opening the door, and, ultimately, letting a friend in.

Place, Level 3 (Distraction)

	DISTRACTION USED	LEVEL OF DURATION AND DISTANCE
Day 1		
Day 2		
Day 3		
Day 4		
Day 5		
Day 6		
Day 7		
Day 8		
Day 9		
Day 10		
Day 11		
Day 12		
Day 13		
Day 14		

Place, Level 4 (Doorbell Counterconditioning)

	VOLUME OF RING	ACTIVITY LEVEL
Day 1		
Day 2		
Day 3		
Day 4		
Day 5		
Day 6		
Day 7		
Day 8		
Day 9		
Day 10		
Day 11		
Day 12		
Day 13		
Day 14		

Knocking People Over

Four on the Floor
Sample plan
Day 1 goals:
- The dog keeps four on the floor when being approached and pet by a very calm person who approaches from a curving path and does not make noise or eye contact.

Day 7 goals:
- The dog keeps four on the floor when approached head-on and pet by a person who talks gently to the dog.

Day 14 goals:
- The dog keeps four on the floor when approached head-on and pet by a person making animated gestures and speaking in a friendly tone.

Day 21 goals:
- The dog keeps four on the floor when approached head-on and pet by an energetic person who has quick movements and an excited tone of voice.

For the chart, write down the actions of the person who successfully greeted your dog without being jumped on. Note the person's tone of voice, speed of moving, gestures, and how directly she approached.

Four On The Floor

	LEVEL OF PERSON'S EXCITEMENT THAT DOG CAN HANDLE
Day 1	
Day 2	
Day 3	
Day 4	
Day 5	
Day 6	
Day 7	
Day 8	
Day 9	
Day 10	
Day 11	
Day 12	
Day 13	
Day 14	

Sit for Greeting
Sample plan
Day 1 goals:
- The dog sees a person across the street. He will sit while you rapid-fire treat-treat-treat. (Then, remove him from the situation with your New Yorker walk, as he's not ready to greet to this person yet.)

Day 7 goals:
- An uninterested person walks by your dog. The dog will sit while you treat-treat-treat.

Day 14 goals:
- An uninterested person walks by your dog. The dog will sit while you treat-pause-pause-treat.
- A friendly person walks by and wants to pet your dog. He will sit while you treat-treat-treat.

Day 21 goals:
- An uninterested person walks by your dog. He will sit while the person passes, and gets one treat at the end.
- A friendly person walks by and wants to pet your dog. He will sit while you treat-pause-treat-pause-treat.

The chart has spaces for two aspects of your training. First, note the characteristics of the passerby: far away and uninterested, approaching head-on and excited to greet your dog, and so on. Additionally, write down how frequently you need to treat your dog to keep him in the sitting position.

Sit for Greeting

	CHARACTERISTICS OF PASSERBY	FREQUENCY OF TREATS
Day 1		
Day 2		
Day 3		
Day 4		
Day 5		
Day 6		
Day 7		
Day 8		
Day 9		
Day 10		
Day 11		
Day 12		
Day 13		
Day 14		

Leash-Walking Problems

Walk with Attention
Sample plan
Day 1 goals:
- Your dog gives you attention while walking around your apartment or house. You reward every time.

Day 7 goals:
- Your dog gives you attention while walking on a quiet street at 6 a.m. You reward with a treat every time.

Day 14 goals:
- Your dog frequently gives you attention while walking on a quiet street at 6 a.m. You reward with a treat 75 percent of the time and praise the rest of the time.
- Your dog occasionally gives you attention while walking on a moderately busy street. You reward with a treat every time.

Day 21 goals:
- Your dog consistently gives you attention while walking on a quiet street at 6 a.m. You reward with a treat 50 percent of the time and praise the rest of the time.
- Your dog frequently gives you attention while walking on a moderately busy street. You reward with a treat every time.
- Your dog gives you attention once while passing delicious street garbage. You reward with a jackpot!

You'll notice that, according to the sample plan, your dog is still working on intermediate-level polite leash walking after three weeks. The first few steps of Walk with Attention usually take the longest to master, but once your dog gets the hang of it, you will likely find that your progress at the intermediate and advanced levels moves much more quickly.

On the chart, note two aspects of your progress: the level of distraction and the frequency of treats (how often and what percentage of the time you are treating). Only start to reduce the treats when the dog has consistently learned Walk with Attention at a certain distraction level over the course of a few days. When in doubt, it is better to overtreat than to undertreat.

Walk with Attention

	LEVEL OF DISTRACTION	FREQUENCY (PERCENTAGE) OF TREATS
Day 1		
Day 2		
Day 3		
Day 4		
Day 5		
Day 6		
Day 7		
Day 8		
Day 9		
Day 10		
Day 11		
Day 12		
Day 13		
Day 14		

Emergency Recall
Sample plan

Day 1 goals:
- The dog responds to your kissy (or other) sound while walking around your home.

Day 7 goals:
- The dog responds to your kissy sound while walking on leash in the presence of a low distraction, such as a noisy car driving by.

Day 14 goals:
- The dog responds to your kissy sound while walking on leash past a mild distraction, such as a squirrel 20 feet away.

Day 21 goals:
- The dog responds to your kissy sound while walking on leash past a moderate distraction, such as a squirrel 10 feet away.
- The dog responds to your kissy sound while sniffing or walking off leash (or on a long line) in an enclosed area with no distraction present.

On the following chart, note the environment in which you practiced Emergency Recall. In particular, note your dog's ability to do Emergency Recall in the presence of bigger and bigger distractions while on your walks.

Desensitize and Countercondition to Triggers
Sample plan

Day 1 goals:
- The dog stays under threshold when he sees or hears a trigger far in the distance, as in down the street. You rapid-fire treat-treat-treat without pause.

Day 7 goals:
- The dog stays under threshold when he sees a trigger across the street. You treat-treat-treat without pause.
- The dog stays under threshold when he sees a trigger far in the distance. You treat-pause-treat-pause-treat.

Day 14 goals:
- The dog stays under threshold when he sees a trigger across the street. You treat-pause-treat-pause-treat.

- The dog stays under threshold when he sees a trigger far in the distance. You treat-pause-pause-treat.

Day 21 goals:
- The dog stays under threshold when he sees a trigger a few feet away. You pull over to the side and rapid-fire treat-treat-treat as the trigger passes.
- The dog stays under threshold when he sees a trigger across the street. You treat-pause-pause-treat.
- The dog stays under threshold when he sees a trigger far in the distance. You give verbal praise and one treat.

Your progress with counterconditioning may take much longer than these examples, but as long as you are seeing progress on a weekly (not necessarily daily) basis, then you're heading in the right direction. On the chart, I recommend writing down every notable attempt to countercondition: both the progress you make and any steps backward you take. By looking at the circumstances surrounding a failed attempt to countercondition, you can learn exactly where your dog's threshold is.

Emergency Recall

	ENVIRONMENT, LEVEL OF DISTRACTION
Day 1	
Day 2	
Day 3	
Day 4	
Day 5	
Day 6	
Day 7	
Day 8	
Day 9	
Day 10	
Day 11	
Day 12	
Day 13	
Day 14	

Desensitize and Countercondition to Triggers

	PROXIMITY TO TRIGGER
Day 1	
Day 2	
Day 3	
Day 4	
Day 5	
Day 6	
Day 7	
Day 8	
Day 9	
Day 10	
Day 11	
Day 12	
Day 13	
Day 14	

Hand Target for Reactivity
Sample plan
Day 1:
  • Indoors, the dog learns the Touch cue from a few inches away.
Day 7:
  • Indoors, the dog can touch your hand from across the room.
  • Outdoors, the dog can touch your hand from a foot away when there are no distractions.
Day 14:
  • Outdoors, the dog can touch from 6 feet away (the full leash length) when there are no distractions. You can use the Hand Target to move him in different directions, such as backward or to the side.
  • Outdoors, the dog can touch from a few inches away when a moderate distraction is present.
Day 21:
  • Outdoors, you can use Hand Target to move the dog backward or to the side to direct him away from a moderate distraction.

For the Hand Targeting chart, record how far your dog has to move to touch your hand (for instance, 6 inches or 6 feet) and what distractions are present.

Leave It
Sample plan
Day 1 goals:
  • The dog can do Level 1 of Leave It while indoors.
Day 7 goals:
  • The dog can do Level 2 of Leave It both indoors and outdoors.
Day 14 goals:
  • The dog can do Level 3 of Leave It indoors.
Day 21 goals:
  • The dog can do Level 3 of Leave It indoors and outdoors.
  • The dog can do Level 4 of Leave It outdoors if you are body-blocking and the temptation is low-value, such as an empty cardboard box.

The chart for Leave It focuses on Level 4 because that level may have several intermediate steps before your dog is truly "fluent" in leaving everything. Pay attention to both the way in which you approach the temptation—whether you are body-blocking or not, and how closely you pass the temptation—and the value (tastiness) of the temptation itself.

Hand Target for Reactivity

	DISTANCE BETWEEN YOU AND DOG	DISTRACTIONS PRESENT
Day 1		
Day 2		
Day 3		
Day 4		
Day 5		
Day 6		
Day 7		
Day 8		
Day 9		
Day 10		
Day 11		
Day 12		
Day 13		
Day 14		

Leave It

	DISTANCE BETWEEN DOG AND TEMPTATION	VALUE OF TEMPTATION
Day 1		
Day 2		
Day 3		
Day 4		
Day 5		
Day 6		
Day 7		
Day 8		
Day 9		
Day 10		
Day 11		
Day 12		
Day 13		
Day 14		

ⓘⓝⓓⒺⓍ

A

acknowledging dog's concern, 55–56
age restrictions, for sports events, 188
agility course, 126–128, 187–189
All Dogs Parkour, 194
alternative behavior, 57–58
animal behaviorists, 28
antlers, as dog treat, 136
anxiety barking, 41
aromatherapy, 143
Association of Professional Dog Trainers
   (APDT), 28
"At the Dog Park" Sternberg, 185
Augustus (Bulldog mix), 193
Azaren, Jude, 194

B

Bach Rescue Remedy, 143
back-clip harness, 87
balance beam, agility training, 127
bark-activated e-collars, 56
barking
   bossy barkers (*See* bossy barkers)
   doorbell drama (*See* doorbell drama)
   out the window (*See* window barking)
   overview, 40–41
   preparation for training, 42
   training tools, 42
Barking: The Sound of a Language (Rugaas), 40
Batman (Chihuahua mix), 6–7, 32, 36, 44–45,
   62, 93, 98–99, 111, 143, 154, 182, 189
Beans (rescue mutt), 44–45, 55, 62, 75, 98, 102,
   106, 120, 122, 139, 143, 147, 154, 182, 194
behavior consultants, 28, 196
behaviorists, 28
bklnmanners.com, 29
body language, 186
body-blocking, 69

boredom, 41, 132
bossy barkers
   Check Me Out, 62–63
   Ignore, 59–61
   overview, 41, 58–59
   Sit for It, 63–64
   That's all, 61–63
Bradshaw, John, 19
Breakfast in Bed, 43–44, 79
Brooklyn Dog Training Center, 7, 45, 186, 189,
   190
bullying, 184

C

CAAB (Certified Applied Animal Behaviorist),
   28
CABC (Certified Animal Behavior Consultant),
   28
canine nose work, 195
canine sports, 186
CBCC (Certified Behavior Consultant Canine),
   28
CDBC (Certified Dog Behavior Consultant), 28
certifications, 27–28
channeling dog's energy, 186
Check Me Out, 33–36, 62–63, 198–199
choke collars, 89
Cindy (Golden Retriever mix), 11
circles, agility training, 127
citronella collars, 56
Clare (Beagle mix), 149
classical conditioning, 105
clicker training, 24
Clothier, Suzanne, 196
collars, 56, 86–89
coprophagia, 179
corrective collars, 89
counterconditioning, 50–54, 108–113, 212, 214
counter-surfing, 21, 22

CPDT-KA or CPDT-KSA certifications, 27
crates, as management tool, 20, 137–142
cues, 23–25, 105

D

DACVB (Diplomate of American College of
  Veterinary Behaviorists), 28
dancing with your dog, 192–193
demand barking, 41, 59
desensitization, 108–113, 212, 214
distracted doggie
    equipment, 86–90
    Hand Target, 97–103
    New Yorker Walk, 90–91
    pulling, 95–97
    Walk with Attention, 91–95
distractions, 26–27
dog parkour sport, 188, 193–194
dog parks, 182–184
dog play, 185
Dog Sense (Bradshaw), 19
dog walkers, 145–148
dog-appeasing pheromones (DAP), 143
Doggie Academy, 6, 21, 24, 112, 187, 188
doggie daycare, 144–145, 183–184
dog's concern, acknowledgment of, 55–56
dog-sport associations, 28
doing nothing, 75
"dominance" style of training, 19
Donaldson, Jean, 196
Don't Shoot the Dog (Pryor), 21
doorbell drama
    Breakfast in Bed, 43–44
    overview, 42–43
    Place, Level 1, 44–47
    Place, Level 2, 48–49
    Place, Level 3, 49–50
    Place, Level 4, 50–54
Down training, 22–23, 163–166
Drop It, 116, 166–169
Dunbar, Ian, 196

E

e-collars, bark-activated, 56
Emergency Drop It, 167–169
Emergency Recall, 105–107, 212, 213
equipment, 86–90, 104–105, 116–118
excitement barking, 41
exercise, 137
extinction burst, 59
eye contact, 32–33, 71, 72

F

fight or flight response, 11–12
Find It game, 148–151
Finn (Pointer mix), 46–47, 92, 96, 124, 129, 162
flat collars, 86, 104
flyball sport, 190–191
force-free training, 28
Four on the Floor, 25–26, 29, 71–72, 206–207
front-clip harness, 87–88, 104, 108

H

Hand Target, 97–103, 113–114, 215, 216
Hank (Labrador mix), 187
harnesses, 87–88
head collars, 88, 104, 108, 116
Heel, 84–85, 160–163
high-value rewards, 17–18, 21
hiring help, 143–148
home alone. *See* naughty when alone
Horowitz, Alexandra, 196
housetrained dogs, 133–134, 176–180

I

IAABC (International Association of Animal
  Behavior Consultants), 28
Ignore, 59–61
instructional videos, 29
International Dog Parkour Association (IDPKA),
  193–194
isolation distress, 132, 151

J

jackpot rewards, 18
jumping on people. *See* knocking people over

K

Kenzi (Miniature Schnauzer), 60
knocking people over
    Breakfast in Bed, 79
    Four on the Floor, 71–72
    Let's Shake On It, 76–79
    New Yorker Walk, 69–71
    overview, 68–69
    Place, 81
    Sit for Greeting, 72–76, 79–81
    Step on the Leash, 70, 71
Kong products, 135, 136
Kontakos, Amanda, 188, 190

L

leash reactivity, 103, 112
leash walking
    distracted dogs (*See* distracted doggie)
    overview, 84–86
    reactive dogs (*See* reactive rascals)
    sidewalk snackers (*See* sidewalk snackers)
leashes
    length, 69, 70, 90
    stepping on, 70, 71
    types of, 89–90
Leave It, 21, 118–125, 215, 217
Let's Shake On It, 76–79
life rewards, 18–19
low-value rewards, 18, 21
Lucy (Bichon Frise), 190

M

Malik Jr. (Bulldog), 63, 65, 100, 111, 155
management versus training, 20–21
marking, 22–24
Martingale collars, 87
massage therapy, 143
McConnell, Patricia, 23, 196

mealtime, 62–63
Michaelis, Jenn, 193
Mickey (Terrier mix), 104
mid-value rewards, 21
Miller, Pat, 196
mind engaging activities, 135–136, 137
Momo (Norfolk Terrier), 115
multiple-dog households, 52
music, for calming, 143
Musical Dog Sport Association, 193
musical freestyle, 192–193
muzzles, 117

N

National Association of Canine Scent Work, 195
naughty when alone
    doggie spa at home, 142–143
    engage the body, 137
    engage the mind, 135–136
    Find It game, 148–151
    hire help, 143–148
    overview, 132–135
    safe areas, 137–142
new behaviors, 17–18
New Yorker Walk, 69–71, 90–91, 116–118
no-reward marker (NRM), 23
North American Flyball Association, 191
nose work, 195
Nylabone products, 135

O

obedience competitions, 16
obstacle course. *See* agility course
Off-leash recall, 170–171
The Other End of the Leash (McConnell), 23
Otttosson, Nina, 135
"over threshold," 104

P

patience, 29
Pauli, Amy, 86
peanut butter, caution about, 42

pet carriers, 171–173
pheromones, 143
piloerection, 186
Place
   Level 1 (duration), 44–47, 200, 201, 202
   Level 2 (distance), 48–49, 200
   Level 3 (distraction), 49–50, 203, 204
   Level 4 (counterconditioning), 50–54, 203, 205
   at outdoor café, 163
   uses for, 21, 81
play groups, 184
Pogo (Goldendoodle), 10–11, 13, 74
positive training, 17, 19, 23, 28
potty, outside or inside, 176–180
predatory drift, 144
prong collars, 89
Pryor, Karen, 21, 196

R

raised hair body language, 186
Rally Freestyle Elements, 192, 193
Rally obedience (Rally-O), 189–190
rawhide caution, 136
reactive rascals
   desensitize and countercondition to triggers, 108–113
   Emergency Recall, 105–107
   equipment, 104–105
   Hand Target, 113–114
   overview, 103
recall, 105–107, 170–171
Reid, Pamela, 196
release words, 23
rescue dogs, 12, 139
resource guarding, 117
retractable leashes, 89–90
rewards, 17–19
rewards-based training, 28
routine behaviors, 18–19, 43, 45, 100, 118
Rugaas, Turid, 40, 196
rural dogs in urban areas, 139

S

safe areas, 137–142, 180–181
safety, sports restrictions, 188
SassyT Canine Academy, 193
sato (Puerto Rican stray dog), 11
separation anxiety, 132–134, 145, 151
sequence for training, 21–23
Shake (or Give Paw), 76–79
side Sit, 158–160
sidewalk snackers
   agility course, 126–128
   equipment, 116–118
   Leave It, 118–125
   New Yorker Walk, 116–118
   overview, 116
Sit, 154–157
Sit for Greeting, 72–76, 79–81, 208–209
Sit for It, 63–64
Sit/Stay, 157
Sit/Stay at street corners, 158–160
social schedule, 176
soiling indoors, 133
spa-like atmosphere for doggies, 142–143
standard leashes, 90
starting training, tips for, 28–29
Step on the Leash, 70, 71
Sternberg, Sue, 185
Susu (Pit Bull), 34, 37, 70, 73, 77, 114, 159, 165

T

T, 28
"teaching an incompatible behavior," 72
Tellington TTouch, 143
term usage, 12
That's all, 61–63
Three (three-legged *sato*), 11–12
tools, 20, 42, 137–142
toys, 135–136
trainers
   locating, 27–28
   professionals, 196
   when to call, 56, 80, 103, 112, 117, 151

training, management versus, 20–21
training plans and charts, 197
treats, 17–19
triggers
    counterconditioning, 108–113
    desensitization, 108–113
    reducing, 55
trips in a pet carrier, 171–173
tying dog outside on streets, 180–181

 U

"under threshold," 108
United States Dog Agility Association (USDAA), 188

V

verbal markers, 22
veterinary behaviorists, 28
video chats, 134–135
videos, instructional, 29

W

Walk with Attention, 91–95, 210–211
walking your dog, 69, 181–182
warm up, training session, 29
Westcott, Sarah, 6, 187
white noise, 55, 143
window barking
    acknowledge dog's concern, 55–56
    alternative behavior, 57–58
    overview, 54
    reduce triggers, 55
World Cynosport Rally Limited (WCRL), 189, 190

X

xylitol, caution about, 42

Y

Yin, Sophia, 196
YouTube, 55, 185

PHOTO CREDITS

ABOUT THE AUTHOR

Kate Naito, CPDT-KA, MS, is a professional dog trainer and the Manners Program Director at Doggie Academy in Brooklyn, New York. A former equestrian, Kate turned her attention to dogs after moving to Brooklyn in 2007. She has written for numerous animal-related publications both in print and online, including Petguide.com and *Equine Journal.*

Kate, a former college instructor, draws upon her background in education to create engaging group classes at the Brooklyn Dog Training Center to address everything from door dashing to sidewalk snacking. Her focus when both training and writing is to provide urban dog owners with force-free training techniques for the real world.

Kate is a rescue advocate and volunteer with a soft spot for senior and special-needs pets. She and her husband share their home with two Chihuahua mixes, Batman and Beans, with whom she participates in dog parkour and other sports. For more information, news, articles, and videos to accompany *BKLN Manners*™ visit www.bklnmanners.com.